ADI RAJ

What You Think Isn't What You Are: Releasing Mental Constructs That Lead to Inner Suffering

Contents

Chapter 1

Introduction

Have you ever felt trapped by your own thoughts? Perhaps you've noticed patterns in your mind—persistent worries, self-judgment, or beliefs about how life "should" be—that seem impossible to escape. Many of us live our lives guided by unseen forces: mental constructs. These constructs are the deeply ingrained beliefs, assumptions, and stories we tell ourselves about who we are, how the world works, and what is possible. Though often invisible, they shape our decisions, relationships, and emotions. Over time, they can become the root of our inner suffering.

The truth is, these constructs are not reality—they are merely filters through which we interpret reality. And the even greater truth is this: what you think isn't what you are.

This book is your invitation to step beyond the mental constructs that have kept you confined. It's a guide to uncover the patterns that no longer serve you, to release them, and to reclaim your innate freedom and peace. It's not about fixing yourself—because you are not broken. Rather, it's about peeling back the layers of untrue beliefs to rediscover the part of you that is already whole and free.

The journey from suffering to inner peace isn't always easy. The constructs we hold are often intertwined with our sense of identity, making it feel as if letting them go means losing ourselves. But this book will show you that what you're letting go of is not your true self. As you release these mental patterns, you'll find clarity, ease, and a deeper connection to who you truly are.

Each chapter of this book is designed to take you step by step from Point A—wanting to change but not knowing where to start—to Point B—knowing exactly what to do to free yourself from the thoughts that weigh you down. Along the way, you'll gain insights, practical tools, and actionable strategies to create lasting transformation.

If you've ever longed for a life where your mind feels like a source of support rather than suffering, this book is for you. Together, we'll explore the power of awareness, the freedom of release, and the peace that comes from living beyond mental constructs.

Your journey to liberation starts here. Let's begin.

Before you begin, take a deep breath and ask yourself: What if the thoughts holding me back aren't true? This book isn't about fixing you, because you're not broken. It's about letting go of beliefs that no longer help you and finding the peace that's already inside. You don't need all the answers right now—just the willingness to explore. As you read, remember: the calm and freedom you're looking for are already within you, waiting to be found. Let this book help guide you to a peaceful, freer life.

Chapter 1: Understanding the Nature of Mental Constructs

The journey to freedom begins with understanding. Before we can release the mental constructs that limit us, we need to know exactly what they are and how they shape our lives. In this chapter, we'll dive into the nature of mental constructs, exploring what they are, how they develop, and why they lead to inner suffering. By the end, you'll have a clear understanding of how your mind works and how you can begin to transform it.

What Are Mental Constructs?

Mental constructs are the mental frameworks or belief systems we create based on our experiences, culture, upbringing, and interactions with the world. They are deeply ingrained patterns of thought, often so automatic that we aren't even aware of them. These constructs act as filters through which we interpret the world and ourselves. They shape our beliefs about what is true, possible, and desirable, but they are not objective truths—they are subjective interpretations that we have come to believe over time.

For example, consider the belief "I'm not good enough." This might stem from childhood experiences, societal expectations, or past failures. It becomes a mental construct, one that the mind holds onto as part of the way we view ourselves, even if it's not grounded in reality. These constructs shape how we approach challenges, how we see ourselves, and how we relate to others.

Examples of Mental Constructs:

- **"I am not worthy"**: This belief might stem from childhood experiences where you were made to feel unimportant or overlooked. As an adult, it shapes how you engage in relationships, how you allow others to treat you, and how you view your own value.
- **"The world is unfair"**: If you've faced injustice or hardship in life, this construct can become a lens through which you interpret every situation. It may lead to feelings of helplessness, frustration, or a sense that you are powerless

to change your circumstances.

- **"Success requires struggle"**: Many people are raised with the belief that nothing worthwhile comes easily. This construct can shape the way we approach challenges—believing that if something isn't difficult, it's not worth pursuing. This can lead to burnout and a feeling of constant dissatisfaction.
- **"People can't be trusted"**: This belief often stems from past betrayals or disappointments. It shapes how we interact with others, causing us to close off emotionally or avoid vulnerability, even when others are trustworthy.

How Mental Constructs Shape Our Perception of Reality

Mental constructs influence every part of our experience. They shape the way we view the world, our relationships, and even ourselves. Since we interpret everything through the lens of these constructs, they become the filter that colors our reality. For example, if we believe that the world is unfair, we are more likely to notice injustices and overlook moments of kindness or fairness. If we believe that we are not good enough, we might constantly seek validation from others or feel inadequate, even when others see us in a completely different light.

This selective perception can reinforce and strengthen our mental constructs. The more we believe something to be true, the more we seek out evidence to support it. This is known as cognitive bias, where we filter out information that contradicts our beliefs and focus on the evidence that confirms them. Over time, this creates a distorted view of reality, keeping us stuck in the same patterns of thought and behavior.

The Origins of Common Mental Constructs

Mental constructs don't appear overnight. They are shaped by a variety of influences throughout our lives. Some of the most common origins include:

1. **Childhood Experiences**: Our early life experiences—especially with family members and caregivers—have a profound impact on the beliefs we form. For example, if a child constantly hears that they are "too much" or "not enough," they might grow up with the mental construct of "I'm not worthy." These early messages shape how we see ourselves and the world around us.

2. **Society and Culture**: Cultural norms and societal expectations can heavily influence the constructs we develop. The belief that "success equals wealth" or "beauty equals happiness" often comes from societal standards and media portrayals. These constructs can shape our goals, our sense of self-worth, and our behavior.

3. **Past Trauma or Painful Experiences**: Negative or painful experiences, such as rejection, betrayal, or failure, can leave lasting imprints on our psyche. These events can lead to the creation of protective mental constructs, such as "People can't be trusted" or "I am unlovable." These beliefs often arise as a way to protect ourselves from future pain, but they end up limiting our growth and happiness.

4. **Learned Behavior**: Mental constructs are also shaped by the behaviors and beliefs we observe in others, especially during our formative years. If we grow up in an environment where success is always associated with hard work and sacrifice, we may internalize the belief that

"work equals suffering" or "happiness is earned through struggle."

As you can see, mental constructs are shaped by many factors and are often deeply ingrained. The good news is that once we become aware of them, we can start to challenge and change them. By doing so, we can begin to see the world and ourselves more clearly, without the distortion of limiting beliefs.

In the next section, we'll dive deeper into how mental constructs create suffering and why they are so difficult to release.

The Role of Mental Constructs in Suffering

Mental constructs have an immense power over our lives, often without us even realizing it. They create the lens through which we interpret the world and, in doing so, they shape our emotional responses and our sense of reality. When we hold onto certain mental constructs—whether they be beliefs about ourselves, others, or the world around us— they can lead to profound inner conflict and suffering. In this section, we'll explore why mental constructs create such conflict, the difference between thoughts and reality, and how these constructs perpetuate our suffering through real-life case studies.

Why Mental Constructs Create Inner Conflict

Mental constructs create inner conflict because they form the foundation of our identity and worldview. Our beliefs about who we are and how the world should work influence how we interact with others, how we make decisions, and how we approach challenges. When our mental constructs are challenged or threatened, we experience tension, confusion, or frustration.

The Conflict Between What Is and What Should Be

One of the core sources of inner conflict comes from the tension between the way things *are* and the way we believe they *should* be. Mental constructs often come with rigid expectations about how life should unfold. For instance, someone who believes that "life should always be fair" will experience inner conflict whenever they encounter injustice or unfairness. The belief that life "should" be a certain way doesn't align with the reality of the world, leading to emotional frustration, anger, and sadness.

This conflict arises because our minds are constantly comparing what is happening around us to the idealized version of reality we've created in our minds. When things don't measure up to that ideal, we suffer. For example, if you hold the belief that "I should always succeed," encountering failure or setbacks can cause feelings of inadequacy or shame. You might experience frustration with yourself or the world for not aligning with your mental constructs of success.

The Role of Cognitive Dissonance

Another reason mental constructs lead to inner conflict is cognitive dissonance. Cognitive dissonance is the mental discomfort we experience when we hold two conflicting beliefs or when our actions contradict our beliefs. This discomfort drives us to either change our beliefs or rationalize our actions to reduce the inconsistency.

For instance, if you believe in the construct that "I must always be in control" but find yourself in a situation where you are unable to control the outcome (such as a relationship or a job), the discomfort of cognitive dissonance can arise. You might feel anxious, stressed, or even angry. In an attempt to resolve the dissonance, you may try to regain control in unhealthy ways or double down on your belief that control is absolutely necessary. This can create a cycle of frustration and inner turmoil, as your beliefs and actions continue to clash.

Attachment to Mental Constructs

We often become attached to our mental constructs because they provide us with a sense of certainty, safety, and identity. When we believe that "I am not good enough," this belief shapes how we interact with the world, often leading us to act in ways that reinforce that belief (e.g., avoiding new challenges, staying in toxic relationships, or not speaking up for ourselves). These constructs offer a sense of control by making the world feel predictable, even if that predictability is built on false or limiting beliefs.

When these constructs are threatened—by experiences or new information that contradicts our beliefs—we experience inner conflict. For example, if you've lived most of your life believing "I must be perfect," the first time you fail or make a mistake, your sense of self-worth may be shaken. This conflict arises because your identity is attached to the belief of perfectionism, and the failure challenges that belief.

Self-Perpetuating Conflict

Mental constructs are often self-perpetuating. Once we internalize certain beliefs about ourselves or the world, we tend to look for evidence that confirms them. This creates a feedback loop where our mental constructs are constantly reinforced, even though they may be causing us pain. For example, if you believe that "people can't be trusted," you might approach new relationships with suspicion, which in turn leads others to behave defensively or distance themselves from you.

Your belief that people can't be trusted is confirmed by the very behavior you are projecting.

This cycle of confirmation bias leads to a deeper sense of suffering because it creates a reality that mirrors our limiting beliefs, which only strengthens our attachment to them.

The Difference Between Thoughts and Reality

A key component of releasing mental constructs and reducing inner suffering is understanding the difference between thoughts and reality. Our thoughts are not objective truths; they are interpretations of our experiences. The mind creates thoughts based on our beliefs, past experiences, and emotional states, but these thoughts do not necessarily reflect the truth about ourselves or the world around us.

The Nature of Thought

Thoughts are like clouds passing through the sky. They arise, linger for a while, and then fade away. However, many people mistake their thoughts for truth. When we think something like "I am unworthy," we often believe it to be a reflection of reality. But in truth, this thought is just a fleeting mental construct, not a fact.

The mind is constantly generating thoughts, but just because a thought arises doesn't mean it is real or true. Many of us identify with our thoughts, thinking that they define us or our circumstances. However, this identification with thoughts creates confusion and suffering. The more we believe our thoughts, the more real they feel, even though they are often based on past experiences or projections about the future—neither of which are accurate representations of the present moment.

Thoughts Are Not Facts

One of the most liberating realizations in the process of releasing mental constructs is that thoughts are not facts. They are simply mental events. For example, the thought "I am not good enough" may arise, but this does not mean that it defines you or reflects your true worth. Thoughts can be challenged, examined, and ultimately released, but only when we recognize them as separate from our true selves.

Reality, on the other hand, is what we experience in the present moment. It is not based on past experiences or imagined future outcomes. Reality is fluid and constantly changing, but our mental constructs often try to freeze it into something static and unchangeable. This is where the suffering arises. When we confuse thoughts with reality, we begin to live in a world shaped by beliefs that no longer serve us.

The Power of Awareness

Awareness is the first step in breaking free from the grip of mental constructs. When we become aware of our thoughts as separate from reality, we can observe them without judgment. This creates a space between the thought and our response to it. Instead of immediately identifying with the thought, we can choose how to respond, whether by letting the thought go or by challenging it.

By practicing mindfulness and awareness, we learn that we are not our thoughts. This realization helps us detach from the inner conflict that arises when we cling to thoughts that create suffering. It allows us to live in the present moment, experiencing life as it is, not as our mental constructs dictate it should be.

Case Studies: How Mental Constructs Perpetuate Suffering

To better understand how mental constructs lead to suffering, let's explore a few real-life case studies. These examples demonstrate how limiting beliefs shape our perceptions and create cycles of pain and frustration.

Case Study 1: Jane's Fear of Rejection

Jane had always believed that she was "not good enough" and that people would reject her if they truly knew who she was. This belief was formed during her childhood when she was often compared to her more outgoing and successful siblings. As an adult, Jane constantly feared that any new relationship—whether personal or professional—would end in rejection. She would avoid putting herself forward for new opportunities, even though she had the skills and abilities to succeed.

This mental construct—rooted in the belief that she wasn't good enough—led to chronic feelings of loneliness, anxiety, and missed opportunities. Jane's fear of rejection kept her stuck in a loop of avoiding connections, which only confirmed her belief that she was unworthy. The more she avoided people, the more isolated she felt, reinforcing her belief that no one would ever accept her.

Over time, Jane came to realize that her belief about herself was a mental construct. She began to challenge the thought "I am not good enough" by seeking evidence to the contrary—such as moments when people showed her kindness, or when she succeeded at tasks she once believed were beyond her reach. By recognizing that her thoughts were not facts, Jane was able to shift her mindset and open herself to new relationships, breaking the cycle of suffering she had been trapped in.

Case Study 2: Mark's Perfectionism

Mark was a perfectionist who believed that "anything less than perfect is a failure." This belief had been ingrained in him by his parents, who placed high expectations on him growing up. As an adult, Mark applied this construct to every aspect of his life. Whether it was his work, relationships, or personal appearance, he constantly felt as though he had to be perfect. The slightest mistake would send him into a spiral of self-criticism, anxiety, and even depression.

Mark's mental construct of perfectionism caused him to feel exhausted and overwhelmed. The pressure to meet impossible standards made him stressed and unhappy. He began to avoid new challenges because he feared failure. This avoidance only led to stagnation and further feelings of inadequacy, reinforcing the belief that he wasn't good enough unless he was perfect.

Through therapy and self-reflection, Mark learned to identify his perfectionist beliefs as mental constructs. By embracing imperfection and reframing failure as an opportunity for growth, he began to experience more peace and acceptance. The release of this mental construct allowed him to approach life with more flexibility, reducing the inner conflict that had once dominated his thoughts.

In the next chapter, we will delve into practical tools and exercises that will help you begin the process of releasing these mental constructs, allowing you to move from a life of inner conflict to a life of clarity and peace.

Awareness: The First Step to Liberation

Awareness is the gateway to transformation. It is only when we become aware of the mental constructs that shape our perception of reality that we can begin to challenge and release them. Awareness gives us the ability to observe our thoughts, beliefs, and reactions without immediately identifying with them, allowing us to distinguish between what is true and what is merely a mental construct. In this section, we will explore how to identify your own mental constructs, the importance of mindfulness and self-observation in this process, and practical exercises to uncover hidden assumptions in your daily life.

How to Identify Your Own Mental Constructs

The first step in releasing mental constructs is to become aware of them. However, mental constructs are often so ingrained in our thought patterns that we don't even realize we are holding them. They feel like truths, but in reality, they are just habitual ways of thinking that we've developed over time. Identifying your own mental constructs is the key to breaking free from their grip.

1. Notice Repeated Patterns in Your Thoughts

One of the easiest ways to identify mental constructs is to observe the recurring thoughts you have about yourself, others, and the world. These thoughts often appear in specific situations and follow a predictable pattern. For example, if you frequently think, "I'm not good enough," this is a mental construct. Similarly, if you often find yourself thinking, "People will always let me down," this too is a construct. The key is to notice thoughts that repeat themselves in various situations or in response to specific triggers.

Ask yourself:

- What beliefs do I hold about myself that keep coming up in different situations?
- Are there recurring thoughts or feelings I have when facing challenges or new experiences?
- What judgments do I make about others that might reflect my own mental constructs?

The more you pay attention, the more you'll begin to recognize these patterns. These recurring thoughts are often rooted in deeper mental constructs that influence your reactions and emotions.

2. Track Your Emotional Reactions

Mental constructs often influence our emotional reactions to events or situations. If you find yourself reacting strongly to something in a way that doesn't seem to match the situation, this can be a clue that there is a mental construct at play. For instance, if a colleague doesn't acknowledge your hard work, and you feel an overwhelming sense of rejection, it may be because you hold a mental construct like "I must always be recognized in order to be valued."

Pay attention to disproportionate emotional responses to minor events. This can help you uncover underlying beliefs that fuel these reactions. For example, if you become anxious at the thought of making a mistake at work, you might have a construct like "I must be perfect to be accepted." Once you identify the pattern, you can begin to recognize it for what it is: a belief that doesn't reflect the truth of who you are or what the situation really is.

3. Examine Your Beliefs About the World and Others

Many of our mental constructs are shaped by how we view the world and other people. If you find yourself consistently thinking in terms of "always" or "never," it's a good indication that you may be holding rigid constructs about how life should be. For example, "People always disappoint me" or "Life is unfair" are generalizations that may reflect a deeper mental construct.

Take some time to reflect on your worldview. Ask yourself:

- What do I believe about people? Do I believe they are trustworthy, or do I expect them to let me down?
- What do I believe about success? Do I think success is earned through struggle, or do I believe it should come easily?
- How do I see the world? Is it a place of opportunity and abundance, or is it a place of scarcity and fear?

By questioning these assumptions, you can start to uncover the hidden beliefs that are guiding your perceptions and experiences.

The Importance of Mindfulness and Self-Observation

Mindfulness and self-observation are essential tools in the process of identifying and releasing mental constructs. Mindfulness is the practice of being present in the moment, paying attention to your thoughts, emotions, and physical sensations without judgment. Self-observation involves stepping back from your experience and watching yourself with curiosity, as though you are a neutral observer.

Mindfulness Helps Break the Cycle of Automatic Thought Patterns

Most of us live on autopilot, reacting to life based on our conditioned beliefs and habitual thought patterns. These patterns are so deeply ingrained that we often don't realize we're operating from them. Mindfulness brings us back into the present moment, allowing us to notice when we are caught up in automatic thinking. Instead of being swept away by thoughts and emotions, mindfulness allows us to observe them as they arise, creating space for choice and awareness.

Mindfulness is not about stopping your thoughts; it's about observing them with non-judgmental awareness. You may notice that your mind constantly jumps to conclusions or repeats negative thought patterns. Instead of getting frustrated with yourself or trying to push these thoughts away, mindfulness invites you to simply notice them without attachment. This observation is the first step in breaking free from mental constructs.

Self-Observation Creates Distance Between You and Your Thoughts

Self-observation helps you create a distance between yourself and your thoughts. Instead of identifying with your thoughts and beliefs, you begin to see them as separate from who you truly are. You are not your thoughts; you are the observer of your thoughts.

When you practice self-observation, you might notice that your thoughts are often based on past experiences or fears about the future, rather than the present moment. This awareness gives you the power to choose which thoughts you want to engage with and which ones you want to let go of.

Self-observation is also key in identifying mental constructs.

As you observe your thoughts, you begin to notice recurring themes or patterns that point to deeper beliefs. For example, you might notice that whenever you feel rejected or criticized, you immediately think, "I'm not good enough," or "I'll never succeed." These thoughts are clues that reveal the mental constructs influencing your reactions.

Exercises to Uncover Hidden Assumptions in Daily Life

Now that we've explored the importance of mindfulness and self-observation, let's look at some practical exercises you can use to uncover hidden assumptions in your daily life. These exercises are designed to help you identify the mental constructs that influence your behavior and emotions, so you can begin to challenge them.

1. The Thought Journal

One of the simplest ways to uncover hidden assumptions is to keep a thought journal. Set aside a few minutes each day to write down your thoughts and feelings. Focus on moments when you experience intense emotions or reactions, especially if they seem out of proportion to the situation.

For example, if you feel angry when a colleague doesn't acknowledge your contribution in a meeting, write down the situation, what you were thinking, and how you felt. Then, ask yourself:

- What belief or assumption is underlying this reaction?
- What does this belief say about me, others, or the world?
- Is this belief true? Can I find evidence that contradicts it?

By journaling regularly, you'll start to notice recurring themes and assumptions that shape your perception of yourself and others. This exercise helps you identify the mental constructs you may not have been aware of, so you can begin to challenge them.

2. The "What if" Exercise

A powerful way to uncover mental constructs is by using the "What if" exercise. This exercise helps you examine your beliefs about the future and challenge the assumptions that may be limiting you.

Take a specific fear or belief you have, such as "I'm not good enough" or "I'll never be successful," and ask yourself:

- *What if this belief isn't true?*
- *What if I am good enough just as I am?*
- *What if success comes from persistence, not perfection?*

By posing these questions, you begin to see that your fears and limiting beliefs are based on assumptions, not facts. This exercise helps you shift from a mindset of limitation to one of possibility and growth.

3. The "Observe Without Judgment" Practice

Mindfulness is a skill that requires practice. One simple exercise you can try is the "Observe Without Judgment" practice. Throughout the day, take moments to pause and observe your thoughts and emotions without labeling them as good or bad. Just notice them as they arise, and let them pass like clouds in the sky.

When you observe your thoughts without judgment, you begin to see that they are fleeting and often don't define who you are. For example, you might have the thought, "I am a failure," but by observing it without judgment, you can recognize it as just a thought, not a truth. This awareness helps you detach from limiting mental constructs and frees you from their influence.

Chapter 2: The Illusion of Identity

In this chapter, we'll dive into understanding identity and how it plays a central role in creating mental constructs that can limit us. We often think of ourselves in a certain way, carrying labels or roles that feel permanent, but in reality, these ideas of who we are are just that—ideas. Identity, as we know it, is an illusion. It's not something fixed or unchanging. It's simply a collection of stories we tell ourselves, influenced by external forces like our upbringing, society, and experiences. When we begin to see these labels for what they are, we can start to free ourselves from their grip.

How Our Identity is Formed

From the moment we are born, we are influenced by the world around us. Our families, schools, friends, and culture all play a significant role in shaping the way we see ourselves. We start to pick up labels like "good" or "bad," "smart" or "dumb," "successful" or "failure," and over time, we begin to identify with these labels. These labels are often not true reflections of who we are, but instead, they are based on the expectations and beliefs of others.

Childhood Influences

Our identity starts to take shape in childhood. As we grow, we learn from our parents, teachers, and peers what is expected of us. If we're praised for being good at math, we might identify ourselves as a "math person." If we are criticized for not being athletic, we might believe we're "not good enough" or "weak." These early experiences can stick with us for a long time, shaping how we see ourselves and how we approach life. Sometimes, we don't even realize that these beliefs are not our own—they are simply what we've been taught to believe about ourselves.

Societal and Cultural Expectations

On top of our family influences, society also imposes certain ideas about who we should be. In many cultures, success is measured by career achievements, money, or social status. If we don't fit into this mold, we may feel like we're failing or missing something. For example, a person who doesn't fit into the traditional idea of success might feel lesser or inadequate. The culture around us reinforces certain roles—like what it means to be a man, a woman, or an adult—and we often take these roles on as part of our identity, even if they don't truly reflect who we are on the inside.

The Self as Roles and Labels

As we go through life, we pick up more roles. We may become "a student," "a parent," or "a professional." These roles become parts of who we think we are. But if we base our entire identity on one role—like being a successful businessperson or a loving parent—we may feel lost if that role is no longer part of our life. What happens when you're no longer in your job, or your kids leave home? Without these labels, you may feel unsure of who you are. The truth is, we are more than just the roles we play in life, but it's easy to forget that when we identify too closely with them.

The Illusion of a Fixed Self

One of the biggest lies we tell ourselves is that our identity is fixed. We think of ourselves as being a certain way—shy, outgoing, smart, or funny—and assume that this is who we will always be. But identity is not set in stone. It's constantly evolving. Our ideas about ourselves change as we grow and learn from new experiences. The illusion of a fixed self keeps us stuck because we cling to the idea that we are defined by what we've been or what we've done.

The Ego's Need for Stability

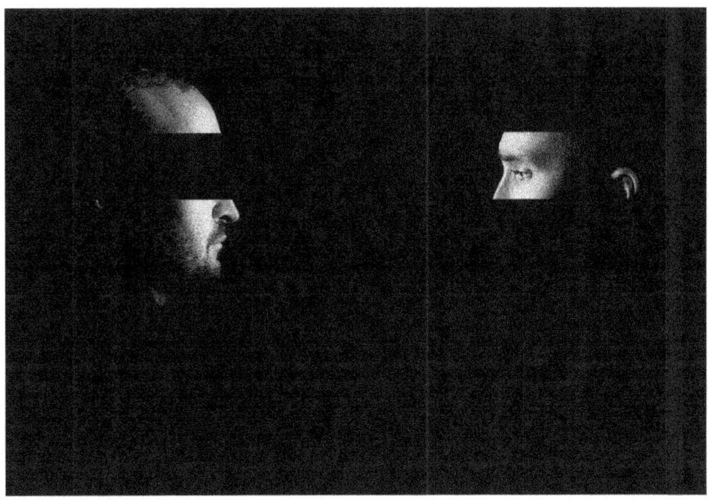

The ego loves stability. It wants to hold onto an identity that it can rely on, something constant to protect itself. This can be comforting, but it also limits our potential. The ego resists change because it fears losing control. It's afraid of stepping into the unknown and letting go of the labels we've clung to for so long. But the truth is, change is inevitable, and embracing it is the key to growing beyond the limitations of our current identity.

The Fluidity of Who We Are

In reality, our identity is fluid, not fixed. We are constantly changing based on our experiences, the people we meet, and the lessons we learn. One day we may feel confident and successful; the next day, we might feel insecure or uncertain. This doesn't mean we've lost our identity—it means we're evolving. Just like a river that changes course over time, our sense of self flows and adapts to the circumstances of life. When we realize this, we stop holding onto a rigid idea of who we are and allow ourselves the freedom to grow into new versions of ourselves.

Personal Growth and Change

Personal growth is all about shifting our identity to better reflect who we truly are. It's about breaking free from the old stories we've told ourselves and embracing a new way of thinking. As we learn and grow, we may start to see ourselves differently. For instance, someone who used to see themselves as "shy" may become more confident and outgoing through personal work. Similarly, someone who once identified with failure can embrace success in a new light. Growth involves letting go of old identities that no longer serve us and stepping into the possibilities of who we can become.

The Impact of Identifying Too Strongly with Our Identity

When we identify too strongly with a particular role or label, it creates limitations. We get trapped in the idea that we must always be a certain way, which causes stress, anxiety, and even suffering. This attachment to a fixed identity is what often leads to inner conflict, because life is full of change, and our identity needs to evolve with it.

Attachment to Roles and Labels

When we identify too much with a role—like "I am a successful lawyer" or "I am a loving parent"—we may fear losing that role or no longer fitting into it. If something happens that shakes our sense of self, such as losing a job or going through a breakup, we can feel like we've lost who we are. We mistakenly believe that our worth is tied to these labels, and this attachment keeps us locked in a limited version of ourselves.

The Fear of Change

The fear of losing our identity is tied to the fear of change. If we see ourselves as a certain type of person—like someone who is always in control or someone who never makes mistakes— we become afraid of anything that challenges that view. We might avoid trying new things because we don't want to be seen as something other than what we've defined ourselves to be. But in resisting change, we miss out on new experiences and opportunities to grow.

The Need for External Validation

Another issue with a fixed identity is that it makes us rely on others for validation. If we see ourselves as "successful" based on our career, we may depend on others to affirm that success through praise or recognition. When we attach our sense of self-worth to external factors like approval or material success, we lose touch with our true value. True self-worth comes from within, and when we stop relying on outside validation, we can finally experience peace and contentment with who we are.

Letting Go of the Illusion of Identity

The path to freedom begins when we let go of the illusion that we are limited by our roles and labels. By releasing attachment to a fixed identity, we create space for a more authentic and fulfilling life.

Question Your Beliefs About Who You Are

Start by questioning the beliefs you hold about yourself. Are they truly yours, or are they simply ideas you've picked up from others? Ask yourself:

- What roles or labels have I attached to myself over the years?
- Do these labels still serve me, or have they become limiting?
- Who would I be without these labels?

These questions help you reflect on how your identity has been shaped by external influences. By seeing these labels for what they are—mental constructs—you can begin to detach from them.

Embrace Change and Uncertainty

To let go of the illusion of identity, embrace the fact that change is a natural part of life. Rather than clinging to a fixed idea of who you are, allow yourself to evolve. Let go of the fear that change will cause you to lose yourself. In fact, it is through change that you discover your true self—beyond the roles and expectations you've been carrying.

Live Authentically

Living authentically means being true to who you are, not based on any label or role. It means letting go of the idea that you have to be a certain way to be accepted or valued. When you stop identifying with fixed roles, you start to live in a way that reflects your true essence—free, creative, and full of potential.

In the next chapter, we'll explore practical tools and practices that can help you let go of these mental constructs, move past the illusion of identity, and embrace the freedom of living from your authentic self.

How We Form Our Sense of Self

Our sense of self is not something we are born with; it is formed over time, through our interactions with the world, the people around us, and our internal reflections. It is the product of many different influences, both external and internal, that come together to shape the person we believe ourselves to be. These influences include the way we are raised, the culture we grow up in, the stories we tell ourselves, and the way we interpret our experiences. Our sense of self is continuously evolving, influenced by our environment, the people we encounter, and our personal growth or lack thereof. In this section, we will explore the role of upbringing, culture, and society in shaping our sense of self, the stories we tell ourselves about who we are, and how our identity can sometimes become a trap.

The Role of Upbringing, Culture, and Society

From the moment we are born, we are exposed to influences that begin to shape our sense of self. One of the primary factors is the environment in which we are raised. Our parents, caregivers, and family members play an important role in teaching us how to navigate the world. The values they instill in us, whether intentionally or unintentionally, influence how we view ourselves and the world around us. For example, children who grow up in families where academic achievement is highly valued might develop a strong sense of self tied to their academic success. In contrast, children raised in environments that prioritize creativity or artistic expression may develop an identity rooted in those pursuits.

Family dynamics are a critical part of this process. For instance, a child raised in an environment where love and approval are conditional on achievements may learn to equate their worth with success. On the other hand, a child raised in a nurturing and supportive environment may grow to have a healthy sense of self-worth independent of external validation. Upbringing is particularly influential because it lays the foundation for the values we adopt and shapes our core beliefs, which influence how we interact with the world.

The culture in which we are immersed plays an equally significant role in shaping our identity. Every society has its own set of norms, values, and expectations that tell us what is acceptable, desirable, and good. These cultural norms can be both empowering and limiting. In many cultures, success is often defined in terms of wealth, status, and material possessions. People are often taught from a young age that their value is tied to these external markers of success. Those who do not meet these cultural standards might feel marginalized or less-than, developing a sense of inadequacy or failure. On the other hand, cultures that prioritize community, family, and social connection might foster a sense of self that values relationships and shared responsibility over individual achievement.

Social influences also impact our sense of self. As we grow older, our interactions with peers, teachers, and mentors contribute to the formation of our identity. Society often imposes roles and expectations on individuals, dictating how they should behave based on factors such as gender, race, socioeconomic status, and profession. These societal expectations can be both explicit, such as laws and regulations, and implicit, such as unwritten rules and social norms. The pressure to conform to these societal standards can be overwhelming, especially when they conflict with our authentic desires or beliefs. We may feel compelled to adopt identities that align with societal expectations, even if they do not resonate with who we truly are.

Ultimately, our upbringing, culture, and society form the framework for how we come to understand ourselves. These external factors influence the way we think about who we are and what we are capable of. They shape our beliefs about our worth, abilities, and place in the world. It is essential to recognize that these influences are not inherently bad, but they can become problematic when we allow them to define us in ways that limit our potential or suppress our authentic selves.

The Stories We Tell Ourselves About "Who We Are"

One of the most powerful forces in shaping our sense of self is the stories we tell ourselves about who we are. These stories are narratives we construct based on our experiences, beliefs, and perceptions. They are the mental frameworks through which we interpret the world and make sense of our existence. The stories we tell ourselves about who we are serve to provide coherence and meaning to our lives, but they can also be limiting, distorting our perception of ourselves and the world.

These personal stories are often shaped by our early life experiences. For example, a child who faces rejection from peers may develop a story that they are "unlikable" or "not good enough." This belief may become an unconscious part of their identity, affecting how they interact with others throughout their life. Alternatively, a person who experiences repeated success in a particular area may develop a story that they are "talented" or "better than others" in that domain. These stories often become so ingrained in our self-concept that they are treated as facts, even though they are based on subjective experiences.

Our stories are often shaped by the external labels placed upon us by others, as well. Society, family, and culture may label us as "successful," "failed," "shy," "outgoing," "good," or "bad," and we often internalize these labels as part of our identity. These external labels can influence the stories we tell ourselves about our worth, capabilities, and potential. For instance, a person who is labeled as "shy" may develop a story that they are inherently introverted and incapable of being outgoing, even if their true nature is more complex.

The stories we tell ourselves can be empowering or dis-empowering. A person who tells themselves that they are a "survivor" may feel empowered by their resilience and strength, while someone who tells themselves that they are a "victim" may feel helpless and stuck in their circumstances. The key to recognizing the power of these stories is understanding that they are not absolute truths. They are simply mental constructs based on how we interpret our experiences. When we cling to a particular story, it can limit our growth and prevent us from exploring new possibilities.

Our stories are not only about the past; they also influence our future. The narrative we have constructed about who we are can shape our goals, aspirations, and decisions. For example, someone who has always seen themselves as "unathletic" may avoid physical challenges or activities, even if they have the potential to excel. Likewise, someone who has defined themselves as a "perfectionist" may avoid taking risks or trying new things for fear of failure. The stories we tell ourselves can create self-imposed limitations that prevent us from embracing new opportunities or stepping outside our comfort zones.

The process of transforming our sense of self involves recognizing the stories we have been telling ourselves and questioning their validity. It requires understanding that these stories are not fixed truths but rather dynamic narratives that can be rewritten. By changing the stories we tell ourselves, we open the door to new possibilities and the freedom to explore different aspects of our identity.

How Identity Can Become a Trap

While identity serves as a way for us to understand who we are and navigate the world, it can also become a trap. When we become too attached to our identity, we limit our potential and create unnecessary suffering. Our identity can become a rigid framework that prevents us from adapting to new circumstances, learning new things, or growing as individuals. This attachment to identity can prevent us from experiencing life fully and embracing change.

The trap of identity often occurs when we become overly identified with a particular role or label. For example, a person who identifies strongly with their profession—such as being a "doctor" or a "lawyer"—may struggle with a loss of identity if they retire or face job loss. Similarly, someone who identifies solely as a "parent" may feel lost or unimportant once their children become independent. When our sense of self is tied to a particular role or achievement, we risk losing sight of who we truly are when that role changes or disappears.

In many cases, identity becomes a trap because it is based on external validation. People often seek validation from others to affirm their identity. This validation may come in the form of praise, recognition, or approval. When we rely on external sources for validation, we tie our worth to what others think of us, which can create anxiety and insecurity. If others do not validate us in the way we expect, we may feel unworthy or inadequate. This constant need for approval can be exhausting and can trap us in a cycle of seeking validation from external sources rather than nurturing self-worth from within.

Another way identity becomes a trap is when it limits our ability to change or evolve. When we become too attached to a particular label or role, we resist change. We fear losing our sense of self if we step outside the boundaries of our established identity. For instance, someone who has always seen themselves as "shy" may avoid social situations out of fear of stepping outside that identity. The same goes for someone who has always been known as "the smart one" in their social circle; they may avoid situations where they might appear vulnerable or make mistakes, for fear of disrupting their carefully constructed identity.

The trap of identity also keeps us stuck in old patterns of behavior and thinking. If we believe ourselves to be a certain way, we tend to act in ways that confirm that belief. For example, someone who identifies as "not good with money" may avoid financial planning or budgeting, reinforcing the belief that they are incapable of managing their finances. This kind of self-fulfilling prophecy keeps us locked in limiting beliefs and prevents us from growing or changing.

Breaking free from the trap of identity requires a willingness to let go of the labels and roles that define us. It involves recognizing that our true essence is not defined by what we do or how others perceive us, but by the unique qualities we possess as human beings. When we release our attachment to identity, we free ourselves from the limitations it imposes and create space for greater personal growth and fulfillment.

In conclusion, our sense of self is formed through a combination of upbringing, culture, societal influences, and the stories we tell ourselves. While identity serves as a tool for navigating life, it can also become a trap when we cling too tightly to it. By recognizing the fluid and evolving nature of our identity, we can free ourselves from the constraints of rigid self-concepts and open ourselves to new possibilities and greater self-awareness.

Breaking Free from Labels

Identity labels, though they may seem harmless at first, often carry powerful implications that can deeply influence the way we perceive ourselves and interact with the world. These labels may have been assigned to us by others or self-imposed based on our past experiences, roles, or achievements. While labels can be helpful in providing structure or a sense of belonging, they can also limit our potential, stifle growth, and restrict our understanding of who we are. To break free from these limitations, we must first recognize the power of labels and understand how they shape our identity. This section will explore how questioning "I am" statements, exploring identity beyond roles and achievements, and engaging in practical exercises can help us redefine our self-concept and liberate ourselves from the constraints of labels.

The Power of Questioning "I Am" Statements

One of the most powerful ways to break free from limiting labels is by questioning the "I am" statements we often use to define ourselves. These statements are deeply ingrained in our consciousness and often serve as the foundation of our identity. Examples of "I am" statements include "I am shy," "I am a failure," "I am not good enough," or "I am a success." These phrases are more than just words; they are declarations of who we believe ourselves to be. They become part of our self-concept and influence how we show up in the world.

While "I am" statements can be empowering in some contexts (e.g., "I am confident" or "I am capable"), they can also limit us by reinforcing negative or narrow self-views. For example, someone who constantly repeats "I am not good enough" may become trapped in a cycle of self-doubt and inaction, which prevents them from taking risks or embracing new opportunities. These labels shape our thoughts, feelings, and behaviors, often without us even realizing it. They create a rigid sense of self that is difficult to break free from, even when circumstances change or we experience personal growth.

The first step in breaking free from labels is to question these "I am" statements. Rather than accepting them as truths, we need to ask ourselves: "Is this really who I am?" "Where did this belief come from?" "Is this label serving me, or is it limiting my growth?" By questioning these statements, we can begin to uncover the underlying assumptions and beliefs that contribute to our sense of identity. For example, if we repeatedly say "I am not good enough," it may be helpful to explore where this belief originated. Did we internalize this message from someone else, such as a parent, teacher, or peer? Or is it based on a past experience that no longer reflects who we are today?

When we question our "I am" statements, we create space for alternative ways of thinking and being. We begin to recognize that our identity is not fixed or predetermined, but rather a fluid and evolving process. By challenging these labels, we can release ourselves from the constraints they impose and open up new possibilities for self-expression and personal growth.

It is important to note that questioning "I am" statements does not mean rejecting or denying the aspects of ourselves that we identify with. Rather, it is about recognizing that our identity is more complex and multifaceted than any single label can capture. We are not limited to one identity or role; we are dynamic, evolving beings with the capacity to change, grow, and explore new dimensions of ourselves. By questioning "I am" statements, we reclaim the power to define ourselves on our own terms.

Exploring Identity Beyond Roles and Achievements

Many of the labels we adopt are tied to external roles and achievements. Society often encourages us to define ourselves by what we do rather than who we are at our core. For example, we might identify as "a teacher," "a doctor," "a mother," or "an entrepreneur," and derive our sense of self-worth from these roles. While these roles can be meaningful and provide a sense of purpose, they can also become limiting if we overly identify with them. When our identity is based solely on our roles or achievements, we risk losing sight of the deeper aspects of who we are.

Exploring identity beyond roles and achievements requires us to look beyond the external markers of success and examine the internal qualities that make us unique. Our worth is not defined solely by our job title, accomplishments, or the roles we play in the lives of others. Instead, our true essence lies in our values, passions, beliefs, and the ways we connect with the world around us.

One way to explore identity beyond roles is by focusing on

our personal values. What do we stand for? What qualities do we admire in others? What brings us a sense of fulfillment and joy? By identifying our core values, we can gain a deeper understanding of who we are at our core. For example, someone who values creativity may feel a sense of loss if their identity is tied solely to a career in finance, even if they are successful in that role. By exploring what truly matters to us, we can begin to redefine our sense of self in a way that aligns with our authentic desires.

Another way to explore identity beyond roles is by embracing the concept of "being" rather than "doing." In our achievement-oriented society, we are often conditioned to value productivity and external accomplishments. We measure our worth based on how much we achieve, how successful we are, and how much we can contribute to society. However, our sense of self is not limited to what we do; it is also shaped by who we are when we are simply being present in the moment. When we shift our focus from "doing" to "being," we create space for self-acceptance and self-compassion, free from the pressure to constantly perform.

Additionally, exploring identity beyond roles involves embracing our imperfections and acknowledging the parts of ourselves that may not fit neatly into societal categories. Society often encourages us to project an image of perfection, but this pursuit of perfection can be stifling. By embracing our flaws, vulnerabilities, and uncertainties, we open ourselves to a more authentic and compassionate understanding of who we are. It is in our imperfections that we often find our true humanity and connection to others.

Breaking free from the confines of roles and achievements is an ongoing process that requires us to continually check in with ourselves and evaluate what is truly important to us. By recognizing that our identity is not defined by what we do or how others perceive us, we free ourselves to explore new dimensions of our being and embrace the fullness of our potential.

Practical Exercises to Redefine Self-Concepts

Redefining our self-concept requires more than just intellectual understanding; it involves practical exercises that help us shift our mindset and reinforce new, empowering beliefs about who we are. These exercises encourage self-reflection, mindfulness, and creativity, allowing us to break free from old labels and create a new narrative about ourselves. Below are some practical exercises that can help us redefine our self-concept and liberate ourselves from limiting identities.

1. Journaling for Self-Discovery

Journaling is a powerful tool for self-exploration and self-reflection. By writing down our thoughts and feelings, we can begin to identify the labels and stories we have been telling ourselves about who we are. Journaling allows us to dig deeper into the beliefs and assumptions that shape our identity. To start, try writing down the following prompts:

- "Who do I believe I am?"
- "What labels have I attached to myself?"
- "How have these labels influenced my actions and decisions?"
- "What is the truth about who I am, beyond these labels?"

As you journal, allow yourself to be honest and vulnerable.

Don't judge or censor your thoughts; simply observe them. Over time, you will begin to notice patterns in the way you view yourself and the limitations imposed by certain labels. This awareness is the first step toward redefining your self-concept.

2. Meditation and Mindfulness

Meditation and mindfulness practices can help us become more aware of our thoughts and beliefs in the present moment. By observing our thoughts without judgment, we can gain insight into the "I am" statements that shape our identity. Try setting aside a few minutes each day to practice mindfulness. Sit quietly and focus on your breath, allowing thoughts to come and go without attaching to them. When thoughts about your identity arise, gently acknowledge them and let them pass. Over time, you will develop the ability to detach from these thoughts and recognize them as temporary rather than fixed truths.

3. Reframing Negative Self-Talk

Negative self-talk often reinforces limiting labels and keeps us stuck in outdated self-concepts. To break free from this cycle, practice reframing negative thoughts by challenging their validity. For example, if you catch yourself thinking, "I am not good enough," pause and ask yourself: "Is this true? What evidence do I have to support this belief? What evidence contradicts it?" Reframing negative self-talk helps us shift from a fixed, limiting mindset to a more flexible and empowering one.

4. Visualization and Affirmations

Visualization is another effective exercise for redefining self-concepts. Take a few moments each day to visualize the person you want to become, free from limiting labels. Imagine yourself living in alignment with your true values, passions, and desires. As you visualize this ideal version of yourself, use positive affirmations to reinforce your new self-concept. For example, "I am worthy of love and success," "I am capable of creating change," or "I am not defined by my past."

5. Creating a New Identity Statement

Finally, create a new "I am" statement that reflects the person you are becoming, free from labels and limitations. For example, instead of saying, "I am a failure," try saying, "I am constantly learning and growing." Rather than "I am shy," say, "I am open to new experiences and connecting with others." By crafting a new identity statement that aligns with your authentic self, you reinforce the belief that you are not defined by past experiences or external labels.

Cultivating True Self-Awareness

Self-awareness is the foundation for personal growth, emotional intelligence, and inner peace. It allows us to understand ourselves at a deeper level, recognizing both the positive and negative aspects of our identity. However, the process of self-awareness can often become muddled due to the influence of the ego, our habitual thinking patterns, and societal conditioning. In this section, we will explore how to cultivate true self-awareness by understanding the difference between the self and the ego, using tools for observing your inner narrative, and establishing daily practices that help us connect with our authentic self. Each step contributes to a deeper understanding of who we are, beyond the mental constructs and limiting beliefs that often hold us back.

Understanding the Difference Between Self and Ego

To cultivate true self-awareness, it's essential to distinguish between the self and the ego. While the ego often represents the part of us that is concerned with status, recognition, and external validation, the true self is the core essence of who we are — our authentic being. The ego is a mental construct that is shaped by our upbringing, culture, experiences, and social conditioning. It operates based on fear, desires, and the need for approval, constantly driving us to achieve, perform, and prove our worth. The self, on the other hand, is not concerned with external recognition or achievement. It is simply aware, calm, and accepting, grounded in the present moment.

The ego often masquerades as the self, making it difficult for us to discern between the two. For example, when we feel pride in our achievements or frustration when we don't receive recognition, we may think these feelings arise from our authentic self. In reality, these emotions are often driven by the ego's need for validation. The ego feeds on labels such as "I am successful" or "I am a failure," and it creates an identity based on these labels. The true self, however, is more expansive and transcendent, embracing both successes and failures as temporary experiences that do not define us.

One of the key aspects of cultivating true self-awareness is learning to observe and separate the ego's voice from the voice of the true self. The ego often speaks in terms of "I need," "I want," or "I must," while the true self speaks in terms of acceptance, presence, and connection. For example, when faced with a challenge, the ego might say, "I am not good enough," while the true self simply acknowledges the situation without judgment, saying, "I am here, I am present, and I will respond as needed."

Understanding the difference between the self and the ego is crucial because it allows us to disengage from the ego's constant need for validation and control. By doing so, we create space for the true self to emerge, enabling us to make decisions that are aligned with our authentic desires and values, rather than out of fear or societal expectations. This awareness is the first step in cultivating genuine self-awareness, which in turn allows us to live more authentically and peacefully.

Tools for Observing Your Inner Narrative

Our inner narrative — the constant stream of thoughts, judgments, and beliefs we hold about ourselves — plays a central role in shaping our sense of identity. Much of this narrative is shaped by our ego, which constantly reinforces the mental constructs that define our self-image. To cultivate true self-awareness, it is important to develop tools and techniques for observing this inner narrative without becoming attached to it.

One of the most effective tools for observing our inner narrative is mindfulness. Mindfulness is the practice of paying attention to the present moment without judgment. By bringing mindfulness to our inner thoughts, we can begin to observe our mental patterns and notice when the ego is influencing our perceptions. For example, if we find ourselves thinking, "I am not good enough" or "I'll never succeed," mindfulness helps us observe these thoughts without becoming entangled in them. Instead of identifying with the thoughts, we learn to simply acknowledge them as passing mental events, much like clouds passing through the sky.

Another tool for observing the inner narrative is journaling. Writing down our thoughts and feelings provides a safe space for self-reflection and introspection. By regularly journaling, we can uncover recurring patterns and beliefs that shape our self-image. For example, when journaling, we may ask ourselves questions like, "What am I feeling right now?" or "What beliefs are underlying my current emotional state?" Writing down our thoughts can help us see our inner narrative more clearly, allowing us to identify limiting beliefs or automatic thought patterns that may be hindering our growth.

Another helpful tool is the practice of self-inquiry, a process of questioning our thoughts and beliefs to uncover their underlying truth. Self-inquiry invites us to ask deeper questions, such as: "Is this belief true?" "Where did this belief come from?" "What evidence do I have to support this belief?" For example, if we find ourselves thinking, "I'm a failure," self-inquiry allows us to explore the root cause of this belief. We might ask ourselves,

"Have I really failed, or have I simply had an experience that didn't meet my expectations?" Through self-inquiry, we can challenge the validity of our negative thoughts and begin to shift our inner narrative toward a more compassionate and empowering perspective.

Additionally, observing our inner narrative through mindfulness, journaling, and self-inquiry allows us to distinguish between the ego's voice and the voice of our true self. The ego is often fueled by fear, judgment, and comparison, while the true self speaks from a place of acceptance, love, and peace. By regularly practicing these tools, we can gain greater clarity and insight into our inner world, helping us cultivate a deeper sense of self-awareness and understanding.

Daily Practices to Connect with Your Authentic Self

To cultivate true self-awareness, it is not enough to simply observe our thoughts and beliefs. We must also engage in daily practices that help us connect with our authentic self, beyond the limitations of the ego. These practices allow us to move from a state of unconscious identification with our mental constructs to a place of conscious awareness and presence. In this section, we will explore several daily practices that can help us reconnect with our true self and deepen our self-awareness.

1. Meditation

Meditation is one of the most powerful tools for cultivating self-awareness. It allows us to quiet the mind, detach from the constant stream of thoughts, and simply be present. By meditating daily, we create a space for stillness and reflection, which allows us to reconnect with our authentic self. During meditation, we can focus on our breath, body sensations, or a specific mantra to anchor ourselves in the present moment. As thoughts arise, we can observe them without attachment, gently returning our focus to the present.

Over time, regular meditation helps us develop a deeper sense of awareness and presence, allowing us to observe our thoughts and emotions without being controlled by them. This practice helps us differentiate between the ego's stories and the truth of who we are. Meditation also promotes mindfulness in daily life, helping us stay connected to our authentic self even in the midst of external distractions.

2. Mindful Breathing

Mindful breathing is a simple but effective practice that can help us stay grounded and connected to our true self throughout the day. By focusing on our breath, we bring our awareness to the present moment, shifting our attention away from the constant chatter of the mind. When we are feeling overwhelmed or caught up in ego-driven thoughts, taking a few deep breaths can help us reconnect with our inner stillness and clarity.

To practice mindful breathing, simply close your eyes and take a few deep breaths, inhaling through your nose and exhaling through your mouth. As you breathe, pay attention to the sensation of the breath entering and leaving your body. If your mind begins to wander, gently bring your focus back to your breath. This practice can be done at any time during the day, whether you're sitting at your desk, walking, or waiting in line.

3. Self-Reflection and Journaling

As mentioned earlier, journaling is a powerful tool for observing and reflecting on our inner narrative. In addition to writing about our thoughts and feelings, we can use journaling as a daily practice for self-reflection. Take a few minutes each day to write down your experiences, emotions, and insights. Ask yourself questions such as, "What did I learn today?" "How did I respond to challenges?" "What beliefs were influencing my actions?" Through self-reflection, we gain a deeper understanding of our motivations, fears, and desires, allowing us to align more closely with our authentic self.

4. Gratitude Practice

Cultivating a daily gratitude practice can help shift our focus from ego-driven desires to appreciation for the present moment. Gratitude helps us recognize the abundance and beauty that already exists in our lives, fostering a sense of contentment and peace. Each day, take a moment to reflect on the things you are grateful for, whether they are big or small. This practice helps us move beyond the constant striving of the ego and connect with the present moment in a deeper way.

5. Affirmations and Positive Self-Talk

Positive affirmations are another powerful tool for cultivating self-awareness and self-compassion. By repeating positive statements, we reprogram our minds and challenge negative beliefs that may be limiting our growth. Affirmations such as "I am worthy," "I am enough," and "I trust myself" help us align with our authentic self and remind us of our inherent value. When we catch ourselves engaging in negative self-talk, we can counter these thoughts with positive affirmations, reinforcing a healthier and more compassionate self-image.

Cultivating true self-awareness is a continuous journey of self-discovery and growth. By understanding the difference between the self and the ego, using tools like mindfulness, journaling, and self-inquiry to observe our inner narrative, and engaging in daily practices such as meditation, mindful breathing, and gratitude, we can reconnect with our authentic self. These practices help us move beyond the limitations of the ego and the mental constructs that define our identity, allowing us to live more consciously and in alignment with our true essence. Through consistent self-awareness, we can experience greater peace, clarity, and fulfillment in our lives, free from the constraints of the labels and beliefs that once held us captive.

Chapter 3: The Emotional Ties That Bind

Our emotional landscape plays a powerful role in shaping who we are and how we experience the world. Emotions, both positive and negative, deeply influence our thoughts, beliefs, and perceptions. They are often the glue that holds our mental constructs together, making it difficult to break free from the stories we tell ourselves. In this chapter, we will explore the emotional ties that bind us to our mental constructs, how these emotional attachments shape our identity, and how we can begin to release them to move toward a more liberated, authentic self.

Emotions are natural responses to events, experiences, and stimuli, but they become more complex when we form attachments to them. Our emotional experiences can become the foundation of our mental constructs, creating a cycle of attachment and suffering. When we experience an emotion, we often begin to identify with it, thinking, "I am angry," "I am sad," or "I am stressed." This is the point where emotions transition from simple feelings to defining aspects of our identity. We begin to believe that we are our emotions, and our emotional state becomes a lens through which we view the world.

This attachment to emotions is often unconscious. For

example, when we face a difficult situation, we might automatically react with anger or frustration, not realizing that we are holding onto a story or belief about ourselves that fuels the emotion. We might believe that we have been wronged, that we are powerless, or that we are not enough. These emotional ties are often formed in childhood, based on early experiences, cultural conditioning, or family dynamics. For example, if we grew up in an environment where emotions like sadness or anger were suppressed, we might learn to associate vulnerability with weakness, making it difficult to express our feelings later in life.

As we continue to experience and internalize emotions, we create patterns that influence our perception of ourselves and the world around us. These patterns are reinforced by our mental constructs, creating an emotional feedback loop. For example, if we feel unloved or unappreciated, we might begin to identify as someone who is unworthy of love, leading to further feelings of sadness or rejection. These emotions become intertwined with our beliefs, creating emotional ties that bind us to an identity that may not be authentic or true.

Emotional attachments often act as anchors, keeping us tied to outdated or limiting mental constructs. When we experience strong emotions, especially negative ones, they tend to reinforce the stories we tell ourselves about who we are. For instance, if we believe that we are not good enough or that we are constantly failing, emotional experiences such as criticism or failure can trigger feelings of shame, guilt, or inadequacy. These emotions then strengthen the belief that we are indeed "not enough," further entrenching the mental construct that has been built around that belief.

These emotional attachments can become so ingrained that

we are no longer aware of them. The emotions become automatic responses to certain triggers, creating a cycle that feels impossible to break. For example, someone who grew up in an environment where love was conditional might carry the belief that they are only lovable when they meet certain expectations. When faced with criticism or rejection, they may react with intense feelings of shame or sadness, which reinforce their belief that they are unworthy of love. The emotional reaction becomes a confirmation of the belief, creating an emotional tie that is difficult to sever.

Emotions also serve as a form of self-protection, reinforcing mental constructs that feel familiar or safe, even if they are not healthy or helpful. For instance, if we have experienced abandonment or rejection in the past, we may develop an attachment to feelings of fear or insecurity, thinking that we need to protect ourselves from future pain. In these cases, the emotional attachment becomes a defense mechanism, keeping us stuck in patterns of behavior that prevent us from growing and evolving.

To break free from these emotional ties, it is essential to recognize how our emotions are interconnected with the stories we tell ourselves about our identity. By observing our emotional reactions and questioning the underlying beliefs, we can begin to unravel the patterns that have kept us trapped.

One of the most powerful ways that emotional ties bind us to mental constructs is through repressed emotions. Repression occurs when we push our emotions down, refusing to acknowledge or process them. This often happens when we perceive certain emotions as "unacceptable" or "weak," based on societal norms or past experiences. For example, a person who has been taught that showing vulnerability is a sign of weakness may repress feelings of sadness, fear, or hurt, believing that expressing these emotions will lead to rejection or criticism.

However, repressed emotions do not disappear; they remain in the subconscious mind, continuing to influence our behavior, thoughts, and actions. When we fail to process our emotions, they often manifest in unhealthy ways, such as anxiety, depression, or physical ailments. Repressed emotions can also contribute to unhealthy patterns of behavior, such as overworking, addiction, or avoidance. For example, someone who has repressed feelings of anger may express this emotion through passive-aggressive behavior, constantly sabotaging their relationships without understanding why.

Repressed emotions are often linked to deep-seated mental constructs that we hold about ourselves. For example, someone who was raised in a household where emotional expression was not encouraged may repress feelings of sadness, equating emotional vulnerability with shame or weakness. This repression creates a mental construct of "I am not allowed to be sad" or "I must always be strong." Over time, this belief becomes internalized, and the person may struggle with expressing their true emotions, even when they are in pain.

In order to break free from repressed emotions and the mental constructs they support, it is essential to create space for self-expression and emotional release. This can be achieved through practices such as mindfulness, journaling, or therapy, where we learn to acknowledge and process our emotions in a healthy and constructive way.

Releasing emotional ties is a process of untangling the emotional threads that keep us bound to limiting beliefs and mental constructs. It requires a willingness to face the emotions that have been buried or ignored, to question the beliefs that have been built around those emotions, and to create new, healthier patterns of emotional response. Here are some steps to help begin this process:

The first step in releasing emotional ties is to become aware of your emotions. This means being present with your feelings, without judgment or avoidance. Instead of reacting automatically, pause and observe the emotion as it arises. Ask yourself, "What am I feeling right now? Where is this emotion coming from? What belief or story is tied to this emotion?"

By observing your emotions with curiosity and openness, you create space for understanding and insight. This practice of emotional awareness helps to disidentify with the emotion, allowing you to see it as a passing experience rather than an aspect of your identity.

Once you have identified the emotion, it is important to examine the beliefs that fuel it. Ask yourself, "What belief is at the root of this emotion? Do I still believe this to be true? Is this belief helping me, or is it keeping me stuck?"

For example, if you feel anger or resentment, explore the belief that may be triggering that emotion. It could be a belief such as, "I am not being treated fairly" or "I deserve more than what I have." Once you identify the belief, you can begin to question its validity and decide whether it is worth holding onto.

Once you have identified the beliefs that are fueling your emotions, it is time to create new emotional responses. This involves consciously choosing to respond to emotional triggers in a healthier, more aligned way. For example, if you are triggered by criticism, you might choose to respond with self-compassion, recognizing that the criticism does not define your worth.

This process takes time and practice, but by consistently choosing healthier emotional responses, you begin to release the emotional ties that bind you to old mental constructs. Over time, this creates new emotional patterns that support your growth and well-being.

Releasing emotional ties also involves embracing vulnerability and allowing yourself to feel and express your emotions. This might mean crying when you feel sad, expressing anger in a healthy way, or allowing yourself to feel fear without judging it. When we allow ourselves to be vulnerable and authentic with our emotions, we create space for healing and growth.

This process of emotional release is deeply personal, and it may take time to fully unravel the emotional ties that bind us to limiting beliefs. However, by practicing emotional awareness, challenging old beliefs, creating new responses, and embracing vulnerability, we can begin to break free from the emotional chains that hold us back and move toward a more authentic and liberated self.

Emotions are a powerful force in shaping our mental constructs and sense of self. They often become the emotional ties that bind us to limiting beliefs, reinforcing the stories we tell ourselves about who we are. To release these emotional ties and move toward a more liberated, authentic self, we must first become aware of our emotions, challenge the beliefs behind them, and create new emotional responses. This process requires patience, self-compassion, and a willingness to embrace vulnerability and self-expression. As we break free from emotional attachments, we create space for greater peace, clarity, and alignment with our true selves.

How Emotions Reinforce Mental Constructs

Emotions are powerful forces that deeply influence the way we perceive ourselves and the world around us. They are not just fleeting reactions to external events, but often become intertwined with the beliefs and stories we hold about ourselves. These beliefs form mental constructs that shape our reality and influence how we approach life. The relationship between emotions and mental constructs is intricate, as emotions not only arise from the mental frameworks we create, but also reinforce and strengthen them. In this section, we will explore how emotions play a significant role in reinforcing the mental constructs that keep us stuck in patterns of behavior, thought, and perception.

The Relationship Between Thoughts and Feelings

At the core of emotional experience is the relationship between thoughts and feelings. Thoughts are often the driving force behind emotional responses, while emotions can, in turn, influence the thoughts we have. This dynamic creates a loop where thoughts fuel emotions, and emotions, in turn, fuel thoughts. For example, if we think to ourselves, "I am not good enough," that thought triggers feelings of inadequacy, fear, or sadness. In response, those emotions might lead us to think more negative thoughts, such as "I will never succeed" or "No one will ever accept me." This cycle creates a self-perpetuating loop where the original thought strengthens the emotional response, which then strengthens the original thought, continuing the cycle.

Our mental constructs—those internalized beliefs about who

we are, what we deserve, and how the world works—are often built on patterns of thought and feeling. Over time, these patterns become ingrained in our psyche, creating a framework through which we experience life. For example, if we hold the belief that we are unworthy of love, we might constantly think about past rejections, betrayals, or moments of loneliness. These thoughts trigger emotions of sadness or fear, which then reinforce the belief that we are unworthy, causing us to further focus on negative past experiences and avoid situations that might challenge this belief.

In this way, emotions act as both the reflection of our mental constructs and the engine that propels them forward. They become both the symptom and the cause of our suffering, as the beliefs we hold influence our emotions, and our emotions influence the continuation of those beliefs. It's important to recognize that emotions are not inherently good or bad. They are simply signals of our internal state, providing us with information about our thoughts and the constructs we've created. When we become aware of this relationship, we can begin to break free from the cycle of negative thinking and emotional reactivity that keeps us stuck.

Why We Cling to Familiar Emotional Patterns

One of the most powerful reasons we continue to cling to familiar emotional patterns is because of the comfort of the known. Even though these emotional patterns might cause us pain, discomfort, or suffering, they are often familiar and predictable. The mind has a natural tendency to resist change, preferring what is known over the uncertainty of the unknown. In many cases, we become so accustomed to certain emotional states that they feel like an integral part of our identity. This attachment to familiar emotional patterns is a major reason why people struggle to break free from limiting mental constructs, even when they are aware that these constructs no longer serve them.

For example, someone who has been raised in an environment where emotional expression was stifled might develop a pattern of suppressing their emotions. Even though this emotional suppression might lead to feelings of frustration, sadness, or resentment, the individual may continue to repress their feelings because it feels safer and more predictable than confronting or expressing them. This emotional pattern becomes a construct that the person relies on to maintain a sense of control or stability. Even though it might lead to emotional numbness or disconnection, the individual often continues to cling to this pattern because it's familiar.

Similarly, someone who has been conditioned to believe that they are not worthy of success or love might repeatedly experience feelings of inadequacy or fear of failure. Although these emotions cause suffering, they are familiar, and the person may feel as though they are an integral part of who they are. This creates a cycle where the mental construct of being "unworthy" reinforces the emotional state of inadequacy, and the emotional state of inadequacy reinforces the belief of unworthiness. The person may not even be fully conscious of the cycle, but they continue to react to situations in a way that perpetuates their mental construct and emotional pattern.

Breaking free from these emotional patterns requires a willingness to step into the unknown. It means confronting discomfort, allowing ourselves to experience emotions that might feel unfamiliar or unsettling, and challenging the mental constructs that we have relied on for so long. This process can be difficult, as it often feels like stepping into uncharted territory, but it is the only way to move beyond the limitations of our old emotional patterns and create a more authentic and liberated way of being.

Recognizing the Emotional Payoff of Mental Constructs

Mental constructs, even the limiting ones, provide us with a certain payoff or reward. This payoff can come in the form of emotional safety, a sense of identity, or a way of coping with the difficulties of life. Recognizing the emotional payoff of our mental constructs is a crucial step in breaking free from them. By understanding the hidden benefits that we derive from these constructs, we can begin to challenge their validity and release their hold over us.

For example, someone who has developed the mental construct of being a "victim" might derive an emotional payoff from this belief. The belief that "the world is against me" or "nothing ever goes right for me" may provide a sense of emotional safety because it allows the person to avoid taking responsibility for their circumstances. It can also elicit sympathy or attention from others, which might provide a temporary emotional boost. This mental construct, although limiting and disempowering, provides a kind of emotional comfort by reinforcing the belief that the person is not to blame for their struggles. The payoff here is a sense of validation and emotional relief from having to take ownership of their life or make changes.

Another example of emotional payoff can be found in the mental construct of perfectionism. The belief that "I must be perfect to be loved or accepted" may drive someone to work harder, be more disciplined, or constantly seek approval. While this mental construct can lead to stress and burnout, it also provides an emotional payoff in the form of external validation or the feeling of control over one's life. For someone who believes they must be perfect, the emotional payoff comes from achieving success, receiving praise, or avoiding the shame of making mistakes. This payoff can make the mental construct feel like a worthwhile trade-off, even though it might ultimately contribute to chronic stress, anxiety, or dissatisfaction.

The emotional payoff of these constructs is often unconscious. We may not realize that our beliefs are serving us in some way until we take a deeper look at the patterns that drive our thoughts and emotions. Once we identify the emotional payoff, we can begin to question whether it is worth maintaining the mental construct that provides it. In many cases, the emotional payoff is no longer serving us in a healthy way, and the mental construct is only perpetuating our suffering.

To begin releasing these emotional payoffs, it is important to recognize the underlying need or desire that the mental construct is fulfilling. For example, if we believe that being perfect is the only way to gain love and acceptance, we might examine the belief that we need to be perfect to feel worthy. Once we recognize that this belief is rooted in a fear of rejection or a need for validation, we can begin to challenge it. We can start to explore the possibility that love and acceptance do not depend on perfection, and that being authentic and vulnerable is a more fulfilling way of connecting with others.

As we become more conscious of the emotional payoffs of our mental constructs, we can gradually release them by embracing healthier ways of meeting our emotional needs. This process involves replacing limiting beliefs with more empowering ones, and learning to meet our emotional needs in ways that are more aligned with our authentic selves.

The relationship between emotions and mental constructs is central to understanding how our internal beliefs shape our experiences. Emotions not only reflect our mental constructs but also reinforce and perpetuate them. Our emotional patterns, though often familiar, can keep us stuck in limiting beliefs that do not serve us. Recognizing the emotional payoff of these constructs and becoming aware of the way emotions fuel and reinforce our thoughts is essential to breaking free from these patterns. By challenging our beliefs and embracing new ways of thinking and feeling, we can release the emotional ties that bind us and move toward greater freedom and self-awareness.

Detangling Emotion from Thought

One of the most transformative skills we can develop in our journey toward inner freedom is the ability to observe our emotions without becoming entangled in them. The connection between thoughts and emotions is powerful, and often, it can be challenging to separate the two. We often confuse our emotional responses with our identity, believing that we are the sum of our emotions and thoughts. In reality, emotions are transient states that arise in response to specific stimuli, while thoughts are beliefs or perceptions that we can change. By learning to distinguish between the two, we can free ourselves from the grip of emotional turmoil and begin to approach life with greater clarity and understanding. In this section, we will explore techniques for observing emotions without judgment, exercises to challenge emotionally charged beliefs, and steps to disentangle past experiences from our current identity.

Techniques for Observing Emotions Without Judgment

The first step toward detangling emotion from thought is to cultivate the skill of observation. When emotions arise, we tend to react automatically, either suppressing them or getting lost in them. Instead of reacting, the goal is to observe the emotions with detachment, as if you were a neutral observer. This allows you to create a space between yourself and the emotion, so you can see it for what it is—a passing feeling that does not define who you are.

One of the most effective techniques for observing emotions is mindfulness. Mindfulness involves being fully present in the moment without judgment or attachment. When an emotion arises, rather than immediately labeling it as "good" or "bad," you simply acknowledge its presence. For example, if you feel anger, you might observe it by saying to yourself, "I notice that I am feeling angry right now." This simple acknowledgment creates space between the feeling and your identity, allowing you to detach from the emotion and see it as something separate from who you are.

Mindfulness also involves observing the physical sensations associated with the emotion. Emotions often manifest in our bodies before we even consciously register them. For instance, anger may cause a tightening in the chest, or sadness might create a heaviness in the shoulders. By paying attention to these sensations, you can develop greater awareness of your emotional responses and create a sense of separation between the emotion and your thoughts about it. By focusing on your breath and the physical sensations in your body, you allow the emotion to rise and fall naturally, without getting caught up in the narrative or judgment that often accompanies it.

Another technique for observing emotions without judgment is to practice self-compassion. Often, we judge ourselves harshly when we experience certain emotions, particularly negative ones. We might think, "I shouldn't feel this way," or "I'm weak for feeling this way." These judgments only serve to reinforce the emotional response, making it harder to move through the feeling. Instead, when an emotion arises, offer yourself compassion and understanding. Remind yourself that emotions are natural and that they don't make you weak or inadequate. By practicing self-compassion, you create an environment where emotions can be experienced without shame or guilt, allowing them to pass through you more easily.

One helpful exercise is to simply sit with the emotion and observe it without trying to change it. Close your eyes, take a few deep breaths, and focus on the emotion itself. Notice where you feel it in your body and how it changes over time. With practice, you'll find that emotions often pass through you more quickly when you don't resist them. The key is to avoid identifying with the emotion or labeling it as something negative. Simply observe, without judgment, and allow the emotion to flow through you.

Exercises to Challenge Emotionally Charged Beliefs

The next step in detangling emotion from thought is to challenge the beliefs that are fueling our emotional responses. Our beliefs are often the root cause of the intense emotional reactions we experience. When we hold onto certain beliefs, particularly those that are emotionally charged, we create a mental construct that perpetuates those emotions. For example, if you believe that you are unworthy of love, any experience that threatens that belief—such as rejection or criticism—will trigger intense feelings of inadequacy or shame. The key to breaking this cycle is to challenge these beliefs and replace them with healthier, more empowering ones.

One powerful exercise to challenge emotionally charged beliefs is the "Cognitive Restructuring" technique, which involves identifying, examining, and reframing limiting beliefs. Begin by identifying a belief that you know triggers strong emotions. For example, you might notice that you feel anxious or angry when you think, "I'm not good enough." Write down this belief and reflect on it: What evidence do you have that this belief is true? Are there instances in your life where you've succeeded or felt accepted? What would happen if you challenged this belief and decided that you are, in fact, good enough?

Next, explore alternative, more empowering beliefs. Instead of thinking, "I'm not good enough," you might replace it with, "I am enough just as I am," or "I am constantly growing and improving." By challenging the belief and replacing it with a more positive affirmation, you create a new mental construct that is more aligned with your authentic self. This exercise helps to break the emotional link between the belief and the associated emotions.

Another exercise is the "Evidence Gathering" method. When you feel a strong emotion tied to a belief, pause and ask yourself, "What evidence do I have that this belief is true?" For example, if you feel anxious before a social event and believe, "I always mess things up in social situations," gather evidence from your past experiences. Are there times when you've had positive interactions with others? Are there examples where you handled a social situation with ease or confidence? By gathering evidence that contradicts the belief, you begin to loosen its grip and weaken the emotional charge attached to it.

It's also helpful to engage in a practice called "thought-stopping." When you notice an emotionally charged thought arising, such as "I'm not good enough," practice interrupting it by saying, "Stop!" in your mind. This simple interruption breaks the cycle of negative thinking and gives you the opportunity to reframe the thought. After saying "stop," replace the negative thought with a more positive, empowering one. For instance, instead of thinking, "I'm not good enough," you might think, "I am worthy of love and respect." With practice, you can begin to create new, more empowering thought patterns that no longer trigger intense emotional responses.

Steps to Disentangle Past Experiences from Current Identity

Our past experiences, especially traumatic or painful ones, can become deeply entangled with our current sense of self. These experiences often form the foundation of the mental constructs we carry with us into adulthood. When we identify with these past experiences, we are unable to see ourselves as separate from them. This creates an emotional tie to the past that continues to shape our present reality. The key to breaking free from this entanglement is to separate past experiences from our current identity, recognizing that while our experiences have shaped us, they do not define us.

One of the most effective ways to disentangle past experiences from our current identity is to practice self-reflection and self-inquiry. Begin by identifying a past experience that still triggers strong emotional responses. For example, you may recall a time when you were rejected or hurt by someone. Notice how you feel when you think about this event—are you still holding onto feelings of anger, sadness, or fear? Now, reflect on how this experience has shaped your identity. Do you believe that because you were rejected, you are unworthy of love? Do you think that because you were hurt, you are doomed to experience pain in the future?

Once you've identified how the past experience has shaped your current sense of self, ask yourself whether it is serving you. Is it empowering or disempowering to continue identifying with this past event? Is it helping you grow, or is it keeping you stuck in the past? Often, we cling to past experiences because they provide a sense of familiarity or security, even if they are painful. We may believe that if we let go of the past, we will lose our identity or sense of self. However, it is only by releasing these past experiences that we can truly embrace our authentic selves and move forward in life.

A powerful exercise to separate past experiences from your current identity is the "Timeline" method. Start by drawing a line on a piece of paper, with the left side representing the past and the right side representing the present. Reflect on key events in your life and place them along the timeline. Notice how certain events, especially painful ones, are still influencing your thoughts and emotions today. As you move through the timeline, notice where you are still holding onto beliefs or emotions tied to these past experiences. Acknowledge these emotions, but remind yourself that they are a part of the past, not your present identity.

To help release these attachments, you might write a letter to your past self, offering compassion and forgiveness for any hurt or pain you experienced. In this letter, remind yourself that while the past shaped who you are, it no longer defines you. By writing this letter, you create a sense of closure and begin the process of separating your current identity from the events that have shaped it.

Another helpful practice is the "Letting Go" exercise, which involves visualizing the past experience as a physical object—such as a ball, a chain, or a box. Imagine that you are holding onto this object, representing the emotional attachment to the past. Now, visualize yourself letting go of the object and watching it float away, symbolizing your release of the past. With each release, affirm that you are not defined by these past experiences and that you are free to create a new, empowering identity moving forward.

Detangling emotion from thought is a critical step in freeing ourselves from the mental constructs that bind us to old patterns of suffering. By learning to observe our emotions without judgment, challenging emotionally charged beliefs, and disentangling past experiences from our current identity, we begin to create the space needed for transformation. This process is not easy, but it is necessary for anyone who wishes to experience true emotional freedom and live a life that is aligned with their authentic self. As we practice these techniques and exercises, we move closer to becoming the person we were always meant to be—free from the past, unburdened by limiting beliefs, and able to respond to life with clarity and wisdom.

The Power of Emotional Release

Emotions are a vital part of the human experience. They serve as signals, guiding us to understanding ourselves and our environment. However, in our society, many of us are conditioned to suppress emotions—especially those we deem as negative, such as anger, sadness, or fear. The tendency to bottle up emotions can have a profound impact on our mental and physical well-being. Suppressed emotions, when not acknowledged or processed, often resurface in unhealthy ways, causing anxiety, stress, depression, or physical ailments. Releasing these emotions in a safe and constructive manner is crucial to healing and achieving inner peace. In this section, we will explore various methods for releasing suppressed emotions, how emotional freedom leads to inner peace, and practical journaling and reflection exercises that can help create emotional clarity.

Methods for Releasing Suppressed Emotions

The process of releasing suppressed emotions is not about simply "letting them go" but about consciously acknowledging and allowing them to move through you. When we suppress emotions, we prevent them from being fully expressed, which can result in them being trapped within our body and psyche. Releasing these emotions requires intentional effort and can be approached from different angles—whether through physical expression, verbal expression, or emotional processing.

One effective method for releasing suppressed emotions is through **somatic experiencing**. This technique focuses on reconnecting with the body, as it often holds the key to understanding the emotions we suppress. Emotions like anger, fear, or grief can create tension and discomfort in the body, manifesting as tightness in the chest, clenched fists, shallow breathing, or a tight stomach. By becoming aware of these physical sensations, we can begin to release the emotions that are trapped. Somatic experiencing encourages a mindful approach to noticing these sensations and gently allowing the body to release them through movement, breathing, or even sound. For instance, if you feel a buildup of tension or anger, you might engage in activities like shaking your body, dancing, or even vocalizing the emotion through shouting or crying. This physical expression can be incredibly liberating, allowing the emotion to be released and processed naturally.

Another powerful method for emotional release is **expressive writing**. Writing down our thoughts and feelings is a simple yet highly effective tool for releasing pent-up emotions. Expressive writing allows us to externalize emotions that might otherwise remain hidden, offering a safe outlet for self-expression. The goal is not to create polished writing but to let the words flow freely from the heart without judgment. This type of writing is particularly useful for emotions like grief, anger, or regret, where we may not have had the chance to fully express ourselves in a healthy manner. By writing about our emotional experiences, we can gain perspective on them, process the feelings, and release any attachment to them. One effective exercise is to set aside time each day to write for a specified period, say 20 minutes, without pausing to censor or judge your thoughts. Let your emotions flow freely, and afterward, reflect on the writing to gain insight and clarity.

Breathwork is another transformative tool for emotional release. Breath is an essential link between the body and the mind, and consciously controlling our breath can help us release trapped emotions. Deep, rhythmic breathing, such as the practice of **holotropic breathwork**, has been shown to induce altered states of consciousness where emotions are brought to the surface. Breathwork involves breathing in a continuous, circular rhythm without pausing between inhales and exhales. This type of breathing can bring suppressed emotions to the surface, allowing the body to process them. When we breathe deeply and consciously, we trigger the body's parasympathetic nervous system, which helps calm the fight-or-flight response and creates space for emotional release.

In addition to breathwork and somatic practices, **guided meditation** is an excellent method for emotional release. Meditation allows us to create inner stillness, which helps us observe our emotions without becoming overwhelmed by them. Through mindfulness meditation, we learn to observe the emotions that arise, without attachment or judgment, and let them pass through us. You can also engage in **compassionate or loving-kindness meditation**, which involves sending love and acceptance to the parts of yourself that hold emotional pain. This practice allows you to create emotional space, releasing tension and inviting a sense of healing and wholeness into your being. When practiced regularly, meditation can increase emotional awareness and cultivate the ability to release emotions in a gentle and nurturing way.

How Emotional Freedom Leads to Inner Peace

When we release suppressed emotions, we create space for emotional freedom. Emotional freedom is not about the absence of emotions; rather, it is the ability to experience and release emotions without becoming overwhelmed or attached to them. The goal is to allow emotions to flow naturally, rather than trying to control or avoid them. Once we begin to let go of the emotional baggage we've carried for years, we experience a profound sense of inner peace.

One of the most significant ways emotional freedom leads to

peace is by reducing the internal conflict caused by unprocessed emotions. Suppressed emotions often create a sense of tension and unease within our minds and bodies. This tension can manifest as anxiety, stress, or even physical illness. When we release these emotions, we allow ourselves to return to a state of balance and harmony. We no longer have to carry the heavy burden of unresolved feelings, and as a result, we feel lighter and more at ease.

Emotional freedom also helps us cultivate **acceptance**. When we resist or suppress our emotions, we are essentially rejecting a part of ourselves. By allowing emotions to flow through us without judgment, we practice self-acceptance. We begin to recognize that all emotions—whether positive or negative—are valid expressions of our humanity. This acceptance allows us to become more compassionate toward ourselves and others, fostering a deep sense of peace and understanding. Instead of viewing emotions as "good" or "bad," we learn to see them as transient experiences that pass in time. This shift in perception helps us let go of the need to control or manipulate our feelings, allowing them to flow freely without resistance.

As we release emotional attachments to the past and stop identifying with our pain, we also make room for **growth**. Emotional freedom enables us to view life with greater clarity and perspective. When we no longer carry the weight of old emotional wounds, we are better equipped to respond to present challenges with wisdom and calm. Our emotional responses become less reactive, and we can navigate difficult situations with a sense of groundedness and peace. This clarity allows us to make decisions that are more aligned with our true desires, rather than being influenced by the emotional baggage of our past.

Furthermore, emotional freedom creates an openness to experiencing **joy** and fulfillment. When we no longer carry the heavy weight of unresolved emotions, we become more attuned to the positive aspects of life. Our ability to experience joy is no longer hindered by emotional blocks. We become more present in the moment, enjoying life as it is, rather than being trapped by the ghosts of past experiences. This newfound sense of freedom invites more peace and contentment into our lives.

Journaling and Reflection Exercises for Emotional Clarity

Journaling and reflection are two of the most effective tools for emotional release and clarity. Writing provides an outlet for expressing emotions that may be difficult to verbalize or even recognize consciously. Through the practice of journaling, we are able to articulate feelings, examine thought patterns, and gain insight into our emotional landscape. This process helps us release trapped emotions and creates space for emotional healing.

One useful journaling exercise for emotional release is called **the Emotional Release Journal**. In this exercise, take a few minutes each day to reflect on your emotions. Write down what you are feeling, without censoring or editing your thoughts. Ask yourself questions like: "What am I feeling right now?" "What triggered this emotion?" "What do I need in this moment?" Let the words flow freely, without worrying about grammar or structure. Afterward, reflect on what you've written. What patterns do you notice? Are there recurring themes or emotions that need to be processed? This practice helps you identify emotional blocks and begin the process of releasing them.

Another powerful journaling exercise is called **The Letter to Your Emotions**. This involves writing a letter to the specific emotion you are currently experiencing. For example, if you are feeling anger, you would write a letter to your anger, acknowledging it and asking it what it needs to be released. The letter might start with, "Dear Anger, I feel you rising within me, and I want to understand you." Throughout the letter, express your thoughts and feelings toward the emotion, offering compassion and acceptance. By acknowledging the emotion and giving it space to be expressed, you allow it to release more easily. After writing the letter, you can either keep it, or if you feel complete, tear it up or burn it as a symbolic gesture of releasing the emotion.

Reflection exercises can also support emotional clarity. One effective method is to engage in **self-inquiry**. Ask yourself deep, introspective questions such as: "What am I really afraid of?" or "Why do I feel so triggered by this situation?" Often, our emotional reactions are tied to underlying beliefs or past experiences. By investigating these triggers through reflective questioning, we can uncover the root cause of the emotion. This process allows us to reframe our thoughts and emotions, enabling us to release them more easily.

Additionally, **gratitude journaling** can be a powerful way to shift emotional energy. When we are focused on what we are grateful for, it's harder to hold onto negative emotions like resentment or sadness. Each day, write down three things you are grateful for, no matter how small. This practice shifts your focus from what you're lacking to what you already have, promoting emotional balance and a greater sense of inner peace.

The power of emotional release cannot be overstated. By learning to release suppressed emotions, we open the door to emotional freedom, which leads to a life of greater inner peace. Through methods such as somatic experiencing, expressive writing, breathwork, and meditation, we can process and release emotions in a healthy way. As we create space for healing, we begin to experience the profound sense of peace that comes with emotional freedom. Journaling and reflection exercises help us gain emotional clarity, identify underlying patterns, and deepen our connection to our authentic selves. With practice, emotional release becomes a powerful tool for living a life that is free from the burdens of the past, allowing us to move forward with greater ease, joy, and peace.

Chapter 4: Rewriting Your Mental Blueprint

Our mental blueprint is the set of beliefs, patterns, and assumptions that shape how we view ourselves and the world around us. These mental constructs are developed over time through our upbringing, culture, personal experiences, and societal influences. In many ways, they form the lens through which we interpret reality. However, these deeply ingrained patterns are not always helpful or aligned with our true desires and values. They often create limiting beliefs, fears, and biases that keep us stuck in unfulfilling situations.

Rewriting your mental blueprint is a powerful way to break free from these constraints and redesign your mind for a more fulfilling and purposeful life. In this chapter, we'll explore the process of identifying outdated or limiting beliefs, replacing them with empowering ones, and creating a mental framework that supports your growth and well-being.

The first step in rewriting your mental blueprint is to identify the limiting beliefs and mental constructs that are holding you back. These beliefs may have been created early in life and have shaped your self-concept and worldview. They are often subconscious, so it's important to cultivate self-awareness and become mindful of the patterns that emerge in your thoughts, emotions, and behaviors.

Start by paying attention to the thoughts that arise in certain situations. Do you have a tendency to doubt your abilities? Do you hold negative beliefs about your worth or potential? These are often signs of limiting beliefs at work. Common limiting beliefs might include thoughts like, "I'm not good enough," "I'll never succeed," "I'm not deserving of love or happiness," or "I'm incapable of change." These beliefs can manifest as self-sabotage, procrastination, or a fear of failure.

To identify these limiting beliefs, it can be helpful to keep a thought journal. Write down the thoughts that come to mind when you face challenges, experience setbacks, or encounter success. Are there recurring themes of self-doubt, fear, or criticism? Once you've recognized these patterns, you can begin to challenge them and replace them with new, more empowering beliefs.

Another effective tool for identifying limiting beliefs is self-inquiry. Ask yourself questions like, "What do I believe about myself in this situation?" or "Why do I feel this way?" By reflecting on the origins of your thoughts and emotions, you can uncover the hidden beliefs that are shaping your reality.

Once you've identified your limiting beliefs, the next step is to challenge them. It's important to recognize that beliefs are not facts; they are simply thoughts that have been repeated and reinforced over time. Many of the beliefs we hold are based on false or outdated information. For example, you might have the belief that you are "not good enough" because of past failures or critical feedback from others. However, this belief does not reflect your true potential or the many successes you've experienced.

To challenge limiting beliefs, begin by questioning their

validity. Ask yourself, "Is this belief really true?" or "What evidence do I have to support this belief?" Often, you'll find that the evidence for your limiting beliefs is weak or non-existent. For example, if you believe you are incapable of succeeding, look at past experiences where you've overcome challenges or accomplished goals. This can help you see that your belief is not an accurate reflection of your abilities.

Another powerful technique for challenging limiting beliefs is cognitive reframing. This involves taking a negative belief and consciously changing the way you think about it. For example, if you believe that failure equals incompetence, reframe the belief to something more empowering, such as, "Failure is a learning opportunity that helps me grow and improve." By reframing your thoughts in this way, you can shift your mindset from a fixed, negative view to a growth-oriented perspective.

Once you've reframed your beliefs, the next step is to replace them with new, empowering beliefs. This involves consciously adopting beliefs that support your growth and align with your values. For instance, if you've been carrying the belief that you are unworthy of success, replace it with the affirmation, "I am worthy of success and I have the skills to achieve it." These new beliefs should be positive, affirming, and rooted in your true potential.

An effective way to reinforce new beliefs is through affirmations. Affirmations are positive statements that you repeat to yourself regularly to shift your mindset. For example, if you're working to overcome self-doubt, you might repeat the affirmation, "I am capable and confident in my abilities." Over time, affirmations help rewire your subconscious mind and replace old, limiting beliefs with new, empowering ones.

Rewriting your mental blueprint requires consistency and practice. Once you've replaced limiting beliefs with empowering ones, you need to integrate these new beliefs into your everyday life. This process involves reprogramming your mind through repetition and mindfulness.

One of the most effective ways to create a new mental blueprint is to engage in visualization. Visualization is a technique where you imagine yourself living in alignment with your new beliefs and goals. For example, if you've adopted the belief that you are capable of achieving success, visualize yourself taking action toward your goals with confidence and ease. See yourself overcoming obstacles, achieving your desired outcomes, and feeling proud of your accomplishments. This helps to reinforce your new mental blueprint and create a sense of self-belief.

Another powerful tool for creating a new mental blueprint is mindfulness meditation. Meditation helps you become more aware of your thoughts and emotions, allowing you to observe them without judgment. Through regular mindfulness practice, you can become more aware of old mental patterns and consciously choose to let them go. As you meditate, focus on cultivating thoughts that align with your new mental blueprint—thoughts of self-compassion, growth, and possibility. Over time, this practice will help reinforce the new beliefs you are working to adopt.

In addition to mindfulness and visualization, it's important to surround yourself with positive influences that support your new mental blueprint. This might involve spending time with people who uplift and encourage you, reading books that inspire personal growth, or listening to podcasts or audiobooks that reinforce the beliefs you are working to cultivate. Your environment plays a significant role in shaping your thoughts and beliefs, so be mindful of the influences you allow into your life.

Creating a new mental blueprint takes time and effort. Old mental constructs have been ingrained in your mind for years, and it will take consistent practice to rewrite them. However, with perseverance and dedication, you can reprogram your mind for success and well-being.

It's important to remember that the process of rewriting your mental blueprint is not linear. There will be times when you fall back into old patterns or doubt your progress. This is normal and part of the journey. The key is to be resilient and keep moving forward, even when it feels challenging. Each time you notice a limiting belief or fall back into old patterns, simply acknowledge it without judgment and return to your new beliefs and practices.

To build consistency, consider setting aside time each day for personal growth practices, such as affirmations, visualization, meditation, or journaling. The more consistently you practice these techniques, the more natural they will become, and the faster you will see results. Celebrate your progress, no matter how small, and remember that every step forward is a victory.

Rewriting your mental blueprint is an empowering process that allows you to break free from limiting beliefs and create a life that aligns with your true potential. By identifying and challenging old, outdated beliefs, replacing them with new, empowering ones, and integrating these beliefs into your everyday life, you can create a new mental framework that supports your growth, well-being, and success. Remember that change takes time and practice, but with dedication and resilience, you can transform your mindset and step into a future filled with limitless possibilities.

Identifying Limiting Beliefs

Our beliefs shape the way we see ourselves and the world around us. They are the mental frameworks through which we process information and navigate life. While some beliefs are empowering and help us achieve our goals, others are limiting. These limiting beliefs can hold us back from reaching our full potential, causing us to live in a cycle of self-doubt, fear, and frustration. The first step toward personal transformation is identifying these limiting beliefs and understanding how they impact our thoughts, emotions, and behaviors.

Common Mental Traps and Their Impact

Limiting beliefs often arise from early childhood experiences, cultural conditioning, or traumatic events. These beliefs can manifest in various forms, such as fear, self-doubt, or perfectionism. Over time, we may become so accustomed to these beliefs that they feel like the truth, even though they do not serve us.

One common mental trap is the **fear of failure**. This belief is rooted in the idea that failure is something to be avoided at all costs. People who struggle with this belief often go to great lengths to avoid failure, even if it means not pursuing their goals or playing it safe in life. The impact of this belief is significant. It creates a fear-driven mindset that limits growth and prevents individuals from taking necessary risks or pursuing their dreams.

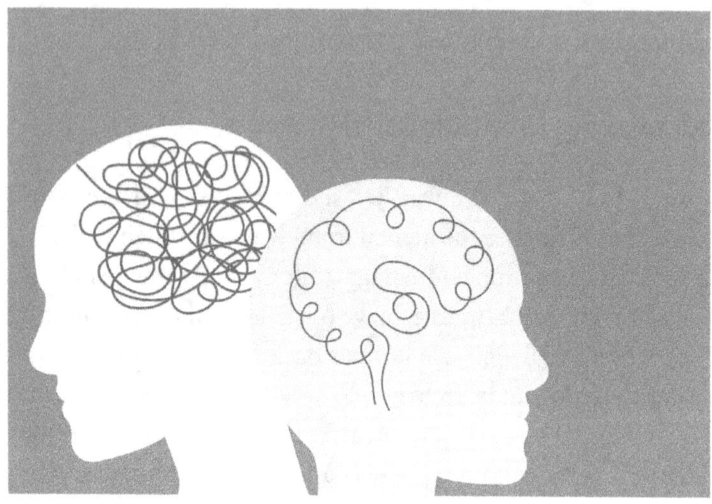

Another mental trap is **self-doubt**, which leads people to question their abilities, worth, and potential. This belief often takes the form of negative self-talk, where an individual constantly tells themselves they are not good enough, smart enough, or capable enough. The result is an overwhelming sense of inadequacy that prevents them from stepping outside their comfort zones and reaching for their goals.

Perfectionism is another limiting belief that often holds people back. The belief that everything must be perfect before it can be shared, completed, or even started can be paralyzing. People who struggle with perfectionism may spend excessive time and energy trying to meet impossibly high standards, leading to burnout, frustration, and missed opportunities.

Other common limiting beliefs include:

- **"I'm not worthy of success or happiness."** This belief often arises from childhood experiences where love or approval was conditional. As a result, individuals may believe they must be perfect or meet certain conditions to deserve success or happiness, leading to feelings of unworthiness.

- **"I can't change."** This belief stems from the idea that who we are is fixed, and there is no room for growth. This belief keeps individuals stuck in old patterns of behavior and prevents them from embracing new possibilities.
- **"I'm not good enough."** This belief creates a sense of inferiority, leading people to feel as though they are always falling short of expectations. It can manifest as chronic self-criticism and perfectionism, preventing individuals from taking action toward their goals.

The impact of these beliefs is profound. Limiting beliefs create a mental barrier that prevents us from living fully. They keep us trapped in a cycle of negative thinking and self-sabotage, which leads to frustration, stagnation, and a lack of fulfillment. The key to breaking free from these patterns is identifying the beliefs that hold us back and confronting them head-on.

How to Uncover Subconscious Beliefs Holding You Back

Many of our limiting beliefs are subconscious, meaning we are not fully aware of them. These beliefs have been ingrained over years of experiences, social conditioning, and personal narratives. To uncover these beliefs, we must engage in self-reflection and develop an awareness of our inner world.

One effective way to uncover subconscious beliefs is through **journaling**. Journaling allows you to explore your thoughts and feelings in a safe, non-judgmental space. Start by writing about any areas of your life where you feel stuck or challenged. What thoughts come up when you think about pursuing your goals or dreams? Are there any recurring themes or negative self-talk? As you write, pay attention to any limiting beliefs that emerge.

Another powerful tool for uncovering subconscious beliefs is **meditation**. Meditation helps quiet the mind and allows us to tune into our inner thoughts and feelings. When we meditate, we create space for insight and clarity to arise. As you meditate, focus on a specific area of your life where you feel limited. Notice any thoughts or emotions that come up. Do you feel fear, doubt, or resistance? These emotions may be connected to a limiting belief that is holding you back.

Self-inquiry is another technique that can help uncover subconscious beliefs. This process involves asking yourself deep, reflective questions such as, "What do I believe about myself in this situation?" or "Where did this belief originate?" Often, the answers will lead you back to past experiences or early childhood memories that formed the foundation of these beliefs.

It can also be helpful to look at **patterns** in your life. Do you tend to repeat certain behaviors or attract similar situations? These patterns are often a reflection of underlying beliefs that are guiding your actions. For example, if you find that you always procrastinate on important projects, it may be a sign of a limiting belief around your abilities or fear of failure. Identifying these patterns can give you valuable insight into the beliefs that are influencing your actions.

Another way to uncover subconscious beliefs is by **examining your emotional reactions**. Our emotions are closely tied to our beliefs. For example, if you feel intense fear or anxiety when faced with a new opportunity, it may be a sign of a limiting belief that is triggering those emotions. Pay attention to the situations that elicit strong emotional responses, as they may point to hidden beliefs that need to be addressed.

Techniques for Confronting Limiting Beliefs Head-On

Once you've identified your limiting beliefs, the next step is to confront them head-on. This process requires courage, self-compassion, and a willingness to question the validity of these beliefs. The key to confronting limiting beliefs is to understand that beliefs are not facts—they are simply thoughts that we've repeated over time.

One of the most effective techniques for confronting limiting beliefs is **cognitive reframing**. Cognitive reframing involves taking a negative or limiting belief and consciously changing the way you think about it. For example, if you have the belief that you are "not good enough" to succeed, you might reframe that belief to, "I am capable of learning and growing, and I have the potential to succeed." Reframing helps to shift your perspective and open up new possibilities for growth and change.

Another powerful technique is **affirmations**. Affirmations are positive statements that you repeat to yourself regularly to replace negative or limiting beliefs. For example, if you have the belief that you are unworthy of success, you might use the affirmation, "I am worthy of success, and I have the skills to achieve my goals." By consistently repeating these affirmations, you rewire your subconscious mind to accept new, empowering beliefs.

Visualization is another technique that can help you confront limiting beliefs. Visualization involves imagining yourself living in alignment with your new, empowering beliefs. For example, if you struggle with the belief that you are incapable of success, visualize yourself taking action toward your goals with confidence and ease. See yourself overcoming obstacles, achieving success, and feeling proud of your accomplishments. Visualization helps to reinforce new beliefs by creating a vivid mental image of what is possible.

It's also important to practice **self-compassion** when confronting limiting beliefs. Many of us hold onto limiting beliefs because we are afraid of failure, judgment, or not being good enough. It's essential to approach this process with kindness and understanding. Remember that you are human, and it's okay to make mistakes and learn along the way. Self-compassion allows you to release the pressure of perfectionism and embrace the idea that you are always evolving.

Another helpful technique is **exposure**. If you have a limiting belief around a specific fear or challenge, exposing yourself to that fear gradually can help you overcome it. For example, if you have a fear of public speaking, start by speaking in front of a small group of friends or family. Gradually increase the size of your audience until you feel more comfortable and confident. Exposure helps desensitize the fear and creates new experiences that challenge the limiting belief.

Finally, **accountability** is an important part of confronting limiting beliefs. Share your journey with someone you trust, such as a mentor, coach, or friend. Having someone to support and encourage you can make the process of confronting limiting beliefs feel less daunting. Accountability also helps you stay on track and continue challenging the beliefs that are holding you back.

In conclusion, identifying and confronting limiting beliefs is a crucial step in personal growth and transformation. By recognizing the common mental traps that limit our potential, uncovering the subconscious beliefs that hold us back, and using powerful techniques like reframing, affirmations, visualization, and self-compassion, we can begin to break free from the constraints of our old mental patterns. With dedication and practice, we can rewrite our mental blueprint and create a life that aligns with our true potential.

Reframing and Restructuring Thoughts

Reframing and restructuring thoughts are fundamental tools for reshaping the way we perceive ourselves, others, and the world. Our thoughts have a profound impact on how we feel and behave. When we change the way we think, we change the emotional landscape of our lives. This transformation allows us to break free from old, limiting beliefs and replace them with healthier, more empowering perspectives. In this section, we will explore key tools for reframing negative thought patterns, how to create empowering mental narratives, and guided exercises to help you rewrite your mental scripts.

Tools for Reframing Negative Thought Patterns

Reframing is the act of changing the way we perceive a situation, event, or thought to see it from a new angle. When we reframe negative thoughts, we challenge their validity and replace them with healthier, more constructive perspectives. Several powerful tools can help us in this process, and incorporating them into your daily life can lead to lasting change.

1. **The ABCDE Model**

The ABCDE Model is a well-known tool used in cognitive-behavioral therapy (CBT) that allows us to break down negative thoughts and reframe them in a more balanced way. This model provides a structured approach to challenging and changing negative thinking. Here is how it works:

- **A (Activating Event)**: The situation or trigger that leads to negative thinking. For example, you might feel nervous before a job interview.
- **B (Beliefs)**: The belief or thought that follows the activating event. You might think, "I'm not qualified for this job."
- **C (Consequences)**: The emotional or behavioral consequences of the belief. This belief may make you feel anxious or avoid practicing for the interview.
- **D (Disputation)**: This step involves challenging the belief. Ask yourself questions like, "Is this belief accurate? What evidence do I have that contradicts this belief?" For example, "I have experience and skills that make me a strong candidate. Just because I'm nervous doesn't mean I'm unqualified."
- **E (Effect)**: The new effect or outcome that comes from disputing the belief. By challenging your limiting belief, you may begin to feel more confident and focused, which helps you prepare better for the interview.

Using the ABCDE model, you can break down negative thoughts into manageable components, making it easier to question and reframe them.

1. Cognitive Distortions

Cognitive distortions are irrational or exaggerated thought patterns that often lead to negative emotions and behaviors. By identifying and challenging these distortions, we can change the way we think about situations and respond more rationally. Some common cognitive distortions include:

- **Overgeneralization**: Viewing a single event as part of a never-ending pattern of defeat. For example, if you fail at something, you might think, "I always fail."
- **Catastrophizing**: Expecting the worst possible outcome in every situation. For example, "If I make a mistake at work, I'll get fired."
- **Personalization**: Taking responsibility for events outside your control. For example, "The team lost because I didn't play well enough."
- **Black-and-White Thinking**: Seeing situations as all good or all bad, with no middle ground. For example, "If I'm not perfect, I'm a failure."

Once you identify these distortions in your thinking, you can reframe them by asking yourself more balanced questions. For example, instead of thinking, "I always fail," reframe it by asking, "What evidence do I have that I've succeeded in the past? How can I learn from my mistakes?"

1. Positive Self-Talk

Self-talk refers to the inner dialogue we have with ourselves throughout the day. Often, this internal dialogue is negative and filled with self-criticism. Reframing negative self-talk is crucial for improving self-esteem and mental well-being. Positive self-talk involves replacing self-critical thoughts with affirmations and constructive statements.

For example, if you catch yourself thinking, "I'm not good enough," reframe it by saying, "I am capable, and I have the ability to improve with effort." Repeating positive affirmations regularly helps rewire the brain to focus on strengths and possibilities rather than limitations.

How to Create Empowering Mental Narratives

Creating empowering mental narratives is essential for overcoming negative thought patterns and embracing a more positive, proactive approach to life. Our internal narratives shape how we see the world and ourselves. When these narratives are empowering, they can fuel confidence, resilience, and a sense of purpose.

1. **Shift from a Victim Mentality to a Creator Mentality**

Many people fall into the trap of seeing themselves as victims of their circumstances. This perspective leads to feelings of powerlessness and helplessness, as individuals believe that external factors control their lives. Shifting from a victim mentality to a creator mentality involves taking responsibility for your thoughts, actions, and emotions.

Instead of thinking, "I can't change my situation," try reframing it as, "I may not have control over everything, but I can choose how I respond and what actions I take." Adopting a creator mentality helps you take ownership of your life and realize that you have the power to create positive change.

1. Focus on Strengths, Not Weaknesses

Many of us focus too much on our perceived weaknesses or failures, which can undermine our confidence and self-esteem. An empowering mental narrative involves focusing on your strengths, talents, and past successes.

Make a list of your strengths and refer to it regularly. Remind yourself of past experiences where you succeeded, overcame challenges, or displayed resilience. This helps you recognize your capabilities and build self-belief. For example, if you've successfully managed a difficult project at work, you might think, "I am resourceful and capable of handling challenges."

1. Embrace Growth and Learning

An empowering mental narrative embraces growth, change, and learning. Instead of viewing mistakes as failures, an empowering narrative sees them as opportunities for growth. This shift in perspective allows you to be more resilient in the face of challenges and encourages continuous self-improvement.

For example, instead of thinking, "I failed at this, so I'm not good enough," try reframing it as, "I made a mistake, but I can learn from it and do better next time." Embracing a growth mindset leads to greater self-compassion and perseverance.

Guided Exercises for Rewriting Mental Scripts

Rewriting mental scripts is a powerful way to change the way we think, feel, and act. These mental scripts are the deeply ingrained patterns of thought that guide our reactions and behaviors. By rewriting these scripts, we can align our mindset with our goals and values.

1. ## The "What If" Exercise

The "What If" exercise involves challenging your negative thoughts by asking yourself questions about the worst-case scenario. Often, we fear the worst outcome, but when we explore these fears rationally, we often realize that they're not as catastrophic as we imagine.

For example, if you're nervous about a presentation, you might ask, "What if I mess up?" Then, reframe it by asking, "What if I make a mistake, but I learn from it and improve next time?" By addressing your fears directly, you can create a more balanced and empowering script for dealing with anxiety.

1. ## Reframing Journal

A reframing journal is a great way to practice restructuring negative thought patterns. At the end of each day, reflect on situations where you experienced negative thoughts or emotions. Write down what happened, how you felt, and what thoughts were running through your mind. Then, reframe those thoughts by challenging their accuracy and offering a more balanced perspective.

For example, if you had a disagreement with a colleague and

felt upset, write down what triggered your emotions. Then, reframe the situation by considering alternative perspectives, such as, "Maybe my colleague had a different opinion, and that's okay. We can still work together." This practice helps you build the habit of reframing negative thoughts and responding more constructively.

1. **Affirmations and Visualization**

Affirmations and visualization are powerful tools for rewiring your mind. Write down a list of positive affirmations that align with your empowering mental narrative. For example, "I am worthy of success," or "I have the strength to overcome any challenge."

Visualize yourself achieving your goals and living the life you desire. Imagine the emotions, the experiences, and the success that will come with living your empowering narrative. Visualization helps solidify the mental shifts you're making and increases your belief in your ability to create the life you want.

Reframing and restructuring thoughts is an ongoing process that requires practice, patience, and consistency. By using tools like the ABCDE model, identifying cognitive distortions, and engaging in exercises like journaling and visualization, you can rewrite your mental scripts and transform the way you think. As you create empowering mental narratives, you will experience a shift in your behavior, mindset, and overall sense of well-being. This process will not only improve your thoughts but also empower you to create the life you desire.

Building a Constructive Inner Dialogue

The inner dialogue we have with ourselves plays a pivotal role in shaping our emotional and mental well-being. It is the internal conversation that reflects our beliefs, self-worth, and perceptions about the world around us. A constructive inner dialogue is empowering, supportive, and optimistic, helping us navigate life's challenges with resilience and clarity. In contrast, a negative or self-critical inner dialogue can limit our potential and lead to feelings of inadequacy, anxiety, and self-doubt.

Building a constructive inner dialogue requires conscious effort and practice. It involves shifting from negative, judgmental self-talk to more positive, encouraging, and realistic thoughts. By doing so, we create a healthier relationship with ourselves, fostering personal growth, confidence, and emotional balance. In this section, we will explore how to build and nurture a constructive inner dialogue that promotes well-being and success.

The first step in building a constructive inner dialogue is **becoming aware of your current self-talk**. Many of us are unaware of the thoughts that constantly run through our minds. These thoughts often go unchecked, influencing our emotions and behaviors without us realizing it. To begin, start observing your inner dialogue throughout the day. Pay attention to the tone, content, and frequency of your thoughts. Do they tend to be negative, critical, or judgmental? Or are they encouraging and supportive? By bringing awareness to your thoughts, you gain the power to change them.

Next, identify and challenge any **negative or unhelpful thought patterns**. Common patterns of negative self-talk include all-or-nothing thinking, catastrophizing, and self-criticism. For example, you might tell yourself, "I always fail," or "I'm not good enough." These types of thoughts can create a sense of hopelessness and defeat, preventing you from taking action or pursuing your goals. Once you recognize these negative thought patterns, challenge them by asking yourself whether they are truly accurate. Are you always failing? Are you truly "not good enough," or is this simply a belief you've internalized? Remind yourself of your strengths, past successes, and the fact that mistakes are part of growth, not evidence of your inadequacy.

Another important step is to **replace negative self-talk with affirmations**. Affirmations are positive statements that reflect the way you want to think and feel about yourself. They are designed to counteract the negative beliefs that may have taken root in your mind. For example, if you struggle with self-doubt, an affirmation might be, "I am capable and worthy of success." If you often criticize yourself for making mistakes, you could say, "I learn and grow from my experiences." Repeating affirmations regularly helps rewire the brain, gradually replacing negative thoughts with more constructive ones.

It's also essential to **practice self-compassion**. Many people engage in harsh self-criticism, holding themselves to unrealistic standards. This type of inner dialogue can be emotionally damaging, leading to feelings of shame and inadequacy. Instead, practice being kind and understanding with yourself, especially during moments of struggle or failure. When you make a mistake, instead of berating yourself, try saying, "I am human, and mistakes are part of the learning process." Self-compassion allows you to accept your imperfections and treat yourself with the same kindness you would offer a close friend.

Reframing negative situations is another key aspect of building a constructive inner dialogue. Life will inevitably present challenges, but how you interpret those challenges can significantly affect your emotional response. Instead of viewing obstacles as insurmountable problems, try to reframe them as opportunities for growth or learning. For instance, if you face a setback at work, instead of thinking, "I'm terrible at my job," you could reframe the situation by thinking, "This is a chance to learn and improve my skills." Reframing helps you maintain a positive outlook, even in difficult circumstances.

One effective strategy for building a constructive inner dialogue is to practice **mindfulness**. Mindfulness involves being present and fully engaged in the moment, without judgment. When you practice mindfulness, you can observe your thoughts without getting caught up in them. This allows you to recognize when negative thoughts arise and gently guide them toward a more positive direction. Mindfulness also helps you stay grounded in the present, rather than getting lost in past regrets or future anxieties. By practicing mindfulness regularly, you can cultivate a more balanced and compassionate inner dialogue.

Lastly, **surround yourself with positivity**. The people, media, and environments we expose ourselves to can influence our inner dialogue. If you spend time with individuals who are critical or negative, it can be difficult to cultivate a positive self-dialogue. Seek out relationships and environments that inspire, uplift, and support you. Read books, listen to podcasts, or engage in activities that promote positivity and growth. By creating a positive external environment, you reinforce your inner dialogue and foster a mindset that encourages self-belief and resilience.

Building a constructive inner dialogue takes time, effort, and patience, but the benefits are immense. As you work to transform your thoughts from negative to positive, you will experience increased self-confidence, reduced stress, and a greater sense of peace. By consciously choosing to engage in an inner dialogue that is kind, empowering, and realistic, you create the foundation for personal growth, happiness, and success. Remember that you are not defined by your thoughts – you have the power to change them, and in doing so, you change your life.

Practices for Fostering Self-Compassion

Self-compassion is the foundation of a constructive inner dialogue. It allows you to treat yourself with kindness, especially during times of difficulty or failure. When you practice self-compassion, you stop engaging in harsh self-judgment and instead replace it with understanding, acceptance, and encouragement. This shift in attitude creates a more supportive and nurturing internal environment, which leads to better emotional resilience and improved mental health.

Acknowledge Your Emotions Without Judgment

The first step in fostering self-compassion is acknowledging your emotions. Often, we tend to suppress or dismiss our feelings, either because we don't want to deal with them or because we've been taught that certain emotions are "weak" or "negative." However, all emotions—whether they are positive or negative—are valid, and acknowledging them is the first step toward self-compassion. Instead of pushing away feelings of sadness, anger, or frustration, take a moment to observe them. Say to yourself, "I'm feeling upset, and that's okay." By accepting your emotions without judgment, you allow yourself to feel and process them fully, rather than getting stuck in denial or avoidance.

Treat Yourself Like a Friend

When we are going through tough times, we tend to be our harshest critics. We often say things to ourselves that we would never say to a friend. Self-compassion involves treating yourself with the same kindness and care that you would offer a loved one. For example, if a friend made a mistake, you would likely offer words of encouragement and understanding. Yet, when it comes to ourselves, we might say, "I'm so stupid" or "I'll never get this right." Replace these self-critical thoughts with supportive and kind phrases, like "I made a mistake, but that doesn't define who I am," or "I am doing the best I can, and that's enough." Practicing this kind of gentle self-talk helps build a more constructive inner dialogue and reduces the impact of negative thoughts.

Practice Self-Forgiveness

Self-forgiveness is another critical aspect of self-compassion. Many people struggle to forgive themselves after making mistakes or experiencing failure. Instead of embracing the lessons from their errors, they ruminate on their shortcomings and let guilt or shame take over. However, self-forgiveness is necessary for healing and growth. Recognize that everyone makes mistakes, and they are an integral part of learning. Once you acknowledge your error, let go of self-blame and focus on how you can do better next time. By forgiving yourself, you release the negative emotional energy attached to your mistakes, allowing you to move forward with greater clarity and peace.

Create Compassionate Rituals

Incorporating self-compassion into your daily life can help reinforce this mindset. One simple way to do this is by setting aside time each day for self-care rituals that nurture your emotional well-being. This could include things like taking a bath, meditating, or practicing deep breathing exercises. Engaging in activities that promote relaxation and well-being helps you reconnect with your compassionate self and counteracts the pressures and stress of daily life. Creating these rituals helps you prioritize your mental and emotional health, leading to a more balanced and compassionate inner dialogue.

Affirmations and Their Role in Reprogramming the Mind

Affirmations are one of the most effective tools for reprogramming the mind. These positive statements, when repeated regularly, can replace limiting beliefs and negative thought patterns with empowering, constructive ones. The power of affirmations lies in their ability to engage the subconscious mind, which drives much of our behavior and perception. When we affirm positive beliefs about ourselves and our abilities, we begin to internalize them, making them an integral part of our mindset.

Understanding the Power of Affirmations

Affirmations are more than just positive statements—they are tools for reshaping the way we think about ourselves and the world. When we repeatedly affirm a positive belief, we send a powerful message to our subconscious mind, reinforcing that belief and integrating it into our core sense of self. For example, if you repeatedly tell yourself, "I am worthy of love and success," you are reshaping the subconscious belief that you are deserving of these things. Over time, this new belief becomes deeply ingrained, influencing your thoughts, actions, and overall mindset.

Creating Affirmations That Align with Your Goals

The effectiveness of affirmations lies in their ability to resonate with your true desires and aspirations. Rather than using generic affirmations like "I am successful," take time to craft statements that are personal and specific to your life. Think about the areas where you feel the most resistance or doubt, and create affirmations that directly address those concerns. For instance, if you struggle with self-esteem, you might affirm, "I am confident in my abilities, and I trust myself to make decisions." By aligning your affirmations with your specific needs and goals, you give them more power and relevance, which leads to more significant results.

Visualization and Affirmations

To further amplify the impact of affirmations, pair them with visualization. Visualization is the practice of imagining yourself experiencing success, happiness, and fulfillment in vivid detail. When you combine affirmations with visualization, you create a mental image of your desired outcome and mentally rehearse the actions and emotions associated with it. For example, if your affirmation is "I am confident in social situations," visualize yourself walking into a room with ease, engaging in conversation, and feeling completely at ease. By mentally rehearsing these scenarios, you condition your mind to believe that this is possible, and you prepare yourself for real-life experiences that align with your affirmations.

Making Affirmations a Daily Practice

For affirmations to be effective, they need to be practiced regularly. The subconscious mind responds best to repetition, so make affirmations a part of your daily routine. Start your day by repeating a set of affirmations aloud or silently, ideally while in a relaxed state. You can also write them down in a journal or incorporate them into your meditation practice. The more consistently you use affirmations, the more they will begin to reshape your inner dialogue and mental framework. Over time, affirmations will replace negative, limiting beliefs with positive, empowering ones, leading to a more constructive and supportive mindset.

How to Cultivate a Supportive Mental Environment

Creating a supportive mental environment is essential for maintaining a healthy, constructive inner dialogue. Our thoughts and beliefs are deeply influenced by the internal environment we cultivate, and by consciously shaping that environment, we can foster emotional resilience, confidence, and positivity. A supportive mental environment encourages growth, creativity, and self-acceptance, and it provides a safe space for learning and healing.

Surround Yourself with Positive Influences

The people, media, and environments you expose yourself to play a significant role in shaping your mental landscape. If you constantly surround yourself with negativity—whether it's from toxic relationships, social media, or the news—it can be challenging to maintain a positive and supportive inner dialogue. Instead, intentionally surround yourself with positive influences that uplift and inspire you. Seek out relationships with people who support your goals and encourage your growth. Limit your exposure to media or environments that trigger negative emotions or reinforce limiting beliefs. By curating your external environment, you create a foundation for a more supportive inner environment.

Cultivate Gratitude

Gratitude is a powerful tool for fostering a positive and

supportive mental environment. When you focus on what you are grateful for, you shift your attention away from negativity and toward the abundance in your life. Start a daily gratitude practice where you write down three things you are grateful for each day. These could be simple things, such as a warm cup of coffee or a kind word from a friend. By regularly practicing gratitude, you retrain your brain to notice the positive aspects of your life, which in turn nurtures a more constructive inner dialogue.

Practice Mindfulness and Self-Awareness

Mindfulness is the practice of being fully present in the moment, without judgment. By practicing mindfulness, you become more aware of your thoughts, feelings, and reactions, which allows you to catch negative or destructive thought patterns before they take hold. Mindfulness helps you cultivate a mental environment that is open, accepting, and non-judgmental, making it easier to create a supportive inner dialogue. Regular mindfulness practices, such as deep breathing, meditation, or simply paying attention to your thoughts throughout the day, help you stay grounded in the present moment and foster a more balanced mindset.

Engage in Self-Care and Reflection

Self-care is an essential component of creating a supportive mental environment. When you take time to care for your body and mind, you send a powerful message to yourself that you are worthy of love, care, and respect. Engage in activities that nourish your body and soul, such as exercise, healthy eating, journaling, or spending time in nature. Self-care allows you to recharge and maintain emotional balance, which supports a constructive inner dialogue. Additionally, regular reflection helps you assess your thoughts and beliefs, giving you the opportunity to identify and challenge any negative or limiting patterns that may arise.

By fostering self-compassion, using affirmations, and cultivating a supportive mental environment, you can begin to build a more constructive inner dialogue. This inner dialogue will guide you toward greater self-acceptance, emotional resilience, and personal growth. With consistent practice, these strategies will become second nature, helping you navigate life's challenges with greater ease and confidence.

Chapter 5: The Path to Inner Stillness

Inner stillness is a state of deep peace and tranquility that allows us to connect with our true selves beyond the noise of the external world and the constant chatter of our thoughts. In today's fast-paced and often chaotic world, finding inner stillness is more important than ever. It's a refuge from the emotional turbulence and mental clutter that often dominate our lives. The path to inner stillness is not a one-time event but an ongoing practice that requires patience, mindfulness, and the willingness to explore and release the mental constructs that prevent us from experiencing peace.

Understanding Inner Stillness

Inner stillness is not about suppressing thoughts or emotions. It is about creating space between you and your thoughts, where you can observe them without becoming attached to them. It's the moment when you no longer identify with the constant mental noise but instead observe it from a place of calm and equanimity. This stillness allows you to experience life in its most authentic form, free from the filters of judgment, fear, and attachment. It is a return to a state of pure awareness—one that exists beyond the stories and labels that we've created about ourselves.

The mind, by nature, is constantly active. It is filled with an endless stream of thoughts, many of which are repetitive, unproductive, or negative. This constant activity can create a sense of mental exhaustion, leaving us feeling overwhelmed and disconnected from our true selves. Inner stillness offers a reprieve from this mental noise, providing clarity and a sense of inner peace. It's the space where you can reconnect with your authentic self and gain a deeper understanding of your true nature.

The Role of Mindfulness in Achieving Stillness

Mindfulness is one of the most effective tools for achieving inner stillness. It involves paying attention to the present moment with full awareness and without judgment. Mindfulness allows you to become more aware of your thoughts, emotions, and sensations, without being swept away by them. Instead of reacting automatically to situations, mindfulness enables you to respond with clarity and intentionality.

By practicing mindfulness, you can begin to create a space between your thoughts and your reactions. You learn to observe your thoughts with curiosity rather than attachment. This practice helps you realize that thoughts are just thoughts— they are not facts, and they do not define who you are. Over time, mindfulness helps you build resilience to external triggers and negative thought patterns, ultimately leading to a greater sense of inner peace.

Mindfulness can be practiced in many ways, such as through meditation, breathing exercises, or simply being fully present in your daily activities. One simple exercise is to sit quietly for a few minutes each day, focusing on your breath. When thoughts arise, acknowledge them, but gently return your focus to your breath without judgment. This practice helps train your mind to stay present and calm, gradually reducing the mental noise that can cloud your mind.

Releasing Mental Constructs

One of the key barriers to inner stillness is the mental constructs we've built over the years. These constructs—our beliefs, judgments, and narratives—shape how we perceive ourselves and the world around us. They often keep us trapped in cycles of anxiety, stress, and inner conflict. These mental patterns are not inherently bad, but when they are left unchecked, they can create a sense of disconnection from our true selves.

The process of releasing mental constructs is essential for achieving inner stillness. By identifying and challenging the limiting beliefs and stories we tell ourselves, we can begin to free our minds from the clutter that prevents us from experiencing peace. This process involves acknowledging the role that these constructs play in our lives and making the conscious decision to let them go.

For example, if you hold the belief that you are not worthy of success or love, this mental construct may manifest as feelings of insecurity or self-doubt. These beliefs keep you stuck in a cycle of fear and avoidance, preventing you from embracing the opportunities and experiences that come your way. Releasing this mental construct involves recognizing that it is not true and that you have the power to redefine your self-worth. As you let go of these limiting beliefs, you create more space for inner stillness to emerge.

Cultivating Acceptance

Acceptance is a critical component of the path to inner stillness. It involves accepting yourself as you are, without judgment or the need to change. This doesn't mean resigning yourself to unhealthy behaviors or situations, but rather, it's about embracing the present moment as it is and acknowledging that everything, including yourself, is enough.

When we resist or reject aspects of ourselves, we create inner tension and conflict. We may resist our emotions, our past, or our circumstances, thinking that we should be different or that things should be different. However, resistance only strengthens the very things we are trying to avoid. Acceptance, on the other hand, allows us to let go of this resistance and make peace with who we are and where we are in life.

Cultivating acceptance starts with self-compassion. Instead of being hard on yourself for not being perfect, learn to embrace your imperfections. Understand that you are a work in progress, and that's okay. As you practice acceptance, you begin to release the need for control and open yourself to the flow of life. This creates a deep sense of inner peace and stillness.

The Power of Meditation

Meditation is one of the most powerful practices for accessing inner stillness. It provides a space for the mind to quiet down and for you to connect with the present moment. There are many forms of meditation, but the goal is always the same: to create a still, calm mind. Meditation helps you observe your thoughts without attachment, allowing them to come and go without identifying with them.

One of the most effective forms of meditation for cultivating inner stillness is mindfulness meditation. In this practice, you focus your attention on your breath, bodily sensations, or a specific point of focus. As thoughts arise, you simply observe them and let them go without judgment. This practice helps train your mind to stay present and calm, creating a deeper sense of stillness and clarity.

In addition to mindfulness meditation, practices such as

loving-kindness meditation or body scan meditation can also promote inner peace. Each type of meditation serves a different purpose, but they all help you connect with your inner stillness and cultivate a sense of peace and presence.

Embracing Silence

Silence is a powerful tool for accessing inner stillness. In a world filled with constant noise and distractions, silence offers a much-needed break for the mind. Spending time in silence allows you to disconnect from the external world and turn inward. It gives you the space to reflect, meditate, and simply be. In silence, you can listen to your inner wisdom and connect with your true self.

Creating moments of silence in your daily life can be transformative. You don't need to go on a silent retreat to experience the benefits of silence. Start by setting aside a few minutes each day to sit in quiet contemplation. Turn off your phone, computer, and other distractions, and simply sit with your thoughts. As you spend more time in silence, you'll find that your mind becomes calmer, and your inner stillness becomes more accessible.

Surrendering to the Present Moment

The final step on the path to inner stillness is learning to surrender to the present moment. We often spend our time ruminating about the past or worrying about the future, which keeps us disconnected from the peace of the present moment. Surrendering to the present moment means letting go of the need to control everything and allowing life to unfold as it is. It involves embracing the uncertainty of life and trusting that everything is happening exactly as it should.

To surrender to the present moment, practice mindfulness and acceptance. Focus on the task at hand and immerse yourself fully in the present. When your mind starts to wander or worry, gently bring it back to the here and now. Trust that you are exactly where you need to be, and that everything will unfold in its own time.

The Value of Silence and Presence

Inner stillness and presence are foundational to personal growth, clarity, and transformation. In a world filled with constant distractions, noise, and demands, the ability to cultivate inner peace is an essential skill for navigating the complexities of life. Inner stillness offers a refuge, a space where you can pause, reflect, and reorient yourself toward what truly matters. Presence, too, is the practice of being fully engaged in the moment, without distraction or judgment. Together, these qualities are essential not only for personal transformation but also for gaining mental clarity, emotional balance, and a deeper connection with your authentic self.

Why Inner Stillness is Essential for Transformation

Inner stillness is at the heart of transformation. It provides a space for you to break free from the mental noise and habitual patterns that shape your reality. In moments of stillness, you create the opportunity to access a deeper part of yourself, beyond the surface-level thoughts and distractions that often dominate your mind. It is in this space that you can observe your mental constructs, limiting beliefs, and unconscious patterns, making it easier to change them.

Without stillness, transformation is nearly impossible because we remain trapped in our old ways of thinking and behaving. We are constantly reacting to external stimuli and our habitual thought patterns, which keeps us in a cycle of sameness. But when we learn to embrace stillness, we allow ourselves to step outside of that cycle and observe our thoughts and emotions from a more neutral perspective. This shift in perception is what facilitates change. Through stillness, we can examine the stories we've been telling ourselves about who we are, what we're capable of, and what we deserve. As we become more aware of these stories, we can rewrite them to reflect our true potential.

Inner stillness is also essential because it fosters deep self-awareness. The more stillness you cultivate, the better you understand your own mind, emotions, and motivations. This awareness is crucial for personal growth because it allows you to identify areas of your life where you may be holding onto outdated beliefs, fears, or unhealthy patterns. Once you become aware of these limitations, you can take steps to release them and make space for new possibilities.

Additionally, stillness creates a sense of peace and calm, which enables you to approach life with a clear, grounded perspective. When you are still on the inside, external challenges become easier to navigate because you're not as easily overwhelmed by stress, anxiety, or reactive emotions. This sense of inner peace supports resilience, helping you stay centered even in the face of adversity.

Overcoming Resistance to Being Present

Being present in the moment is often easier said than done. Many of us find it challenging to be fully present, and this resistance stems from a variety of sources. Some people resist presence because they fear the stillness that comes with it. When we stop to pause, we are often confronted with our own emotions, thoughts, and unresolved issues. These can feel uncomfortable, so our natural tendency is to avoid them. Distractions such as work, social media, or even the busyness of our daily lives provide an easy escape from having to confront the discomfort of stillness.

In other cases, resistance to being present may come from a fear of missing out (FOMO) or the anxiety that comes with worrying about the future. When our minds are consumed with thoughts about what might happen next or the mistakes of the past, it becomes difficult to focus on what is happening in the present moment. We become so caught up in planning, problem-solving, or replaying events that we miss the beauty and richness of the current moment. This resistance can also stem from societal conditioning, which often values constant productivity, achievement, and forward momentum over rest and reflection.

Overcoming resistance to being present requires a shift in mindset. First, it's important to recognize that presence doesn't mean ignoring responsibilities or avoiding challenges. Being present means fully engaging with whatever is happening in the moment—whether that's a conversation, a task, or an emotional experience—without being lost in thought or distracted by external stimuli. It's about giving your full attention to the here and now.

One of the most effective ways to overcome resistance to being present is through mindfulness practices. Mindfulness encourages you to observe your thoughts, feelings, and sensations without judgment or attachment. By simply noticing what is happening in your mind and body, you create a sense of detachment from the constant stream of thoughts and emotions. This detachment allows you to experience the present moment without becoming overwhelmed or reactive. With regular practice, you can learn to cultivate a sense of peace and acceptance, even in the face of discomfort.

It's also helpful to recognize that being present is not about achieving a state of perfection or stillness, but rather about being open to whatever arises in the moment. There will be times when your mind wanders, and that's okay. The key is to gently bring your focus back to the present without judgment. Each time you return to the present moment, you strengthen your ability to stay grounded and calm, no matter what's happening around you.

The Relationship Between Stillness and Mental Clarity

The relationship between stillness and mental clarity is deeply interconnected. In today's world, our minds are constantly bombarded with information, stimuli, and demands, making it difficult to think clearly. The constant chatter in our minds often leads to confusion, stress, and an inability to focus. Stillness, however, offers a solution to this mental clutter. When we make space for stillness, we can quiet the mental noise and gain clarity on what matters most.

When the mind is still, it is like a calm pond. The surface reflects reality clearly because there are no ripples or disturbances to cloud the vision. Similarly, when we cultivate stillness in our minds, we can perceive situations more objectively and make decisions with greater clarity. Stillness allows us to step back from the noise of our thoughts and examine things with a fresh perspective.

One of the primary benefits of stillness is that it helps to remove the mental fog that can arise from stress, anxiety, or overthinking. When we are in a state of constant mental activity, it becomes difficult to see things clearly. Our judgments become clouded by emotions, past experiences, and limiting beliefs. But in stillness, we have the space to observe our thoughts from a neutral standpoint. This clarity enables us to see things as they truly are, without the distortions created by fear or bias.

Stillness also helps to sharpen our focus. When we are constantly distracted by external noise or internal chatter, it becomes difficult to concentrate on the task at hand. In contrast, when we create moments of stillness throughout the day, we allow our minds to reset and recharge. This renewed clarity enhances our ability to focus and engage fully in whatever we are doing, whether it's working on a project, engaging in a conversation, or reflecting on our personal growth.

Additionally, stillness enhances our intuition. When we quiet the mind, we open ourselves to subtle insights and guidance that are often drowned out by mental noise. Many people find that they make better decisions or experience moments of inspiration when they are in a calm, still state. By allowing ourselves to be present and still, we create the conditions for intuitive wisdom to emerge.

The value of silence and presence cannot be overstated. Inner stillness is not only essential for personal transformation, but it is also the key to accessing mental clarity, emotional balance, and authentic self-awareness. In a world that constantly demands our attention, taking time to cultivate stillness and presence is a radical act of self-care. It allows us to connect more deeply with ourselves and with the world around us. It provides the mental clarity we need to make decisions that align with our true desires and purpose.

Overcoming resistance to being present is an ongoing process that requires patience and mindfulness. By embracing the present moment with openness and curiosity, we can move beyond the distractions and fears that keep us from experiencing life fully. As we develop a practice of stillness, we gain access to a deeper sense of peace, clarity, and insight, which supports us on our journey toward personal growth and transformation.

In the quiet space of stillness, we can hear the whispers of our intuition, feel the depths of our emotions, and connect with the essence of who we truly are. It is in this space that transformation occurs, and it is in this space that we can find the clarity and peace that we have been searching for all along.

Practices for Cultivating Presence

In the fast-paced, often overwhelming world we live in, cultivating presence can be a profound antidote to stress and distraction. Being present doesn't mean simply being physically in the moment; it requires engaging fully with the here and now, connecting to both your internal and external environment without judgment or distraction. This practice leads to deeper self-awareness, greater mental clarity, and a sense of peace. Here, we will explore several powerful practices to help you cultivate presence in your life: guided meditations, grounding techniques, and breathwork.

Guided Meditations for Awareness and Detachment

Guided meditation is an excellent tool for fostering presence because it offers a structured approach to quiet the mind, focus attention, and cultivate mindfulness. During a guided meditation, you are led through a process of calming your thoughts, tuning into your body, and observing your mental and emotional state. By practicing regularly, you can train your mind to become more aware and less reactive, helping you to stay grounded and present in the moment.

The primary goal of guided meditation is to foster awareness and detachment from your thoughts, emotions, and external distractions. Often, our minds are dominated by a constant flow of thoughts—whether worries about the future, regrets from the past, or judgments about the present. These mental distractions prevent us from truly engaging with the current moment. Through guided meditation, you learn to observe these thoughts without identifying with them, creating space between yourself and your mental noise.

A typical guided meditation for awareness and detachment might start with a few deep breaths to help relax your body and mind. The guide will then encourage you to bring attention to the present moment, often by focusing on bodily sensations like the feeling of your feet on the ground or the rhythm of your breath. As thoughts arise, the guide will remind you to acknowledge them and then gently return your focus to the breath or your surroundings.

This practice of gently letting go of distractions and returning to the present moment helps to cultivate mindfulness. The more you practice, the more adept you become at noticing when your mind has wandered and gently guiding it back. The process of detaching from thoughts is vital for cultivating a sense of presence because it allows you to experience life as it truly is, rather than through the filter of past experiences or future anxieties.

Over time, guided meditation also helps you develop the skill of emotional detachment. When emotions arise—whether positive or negative—you begin to notice them without immediately reacting to them. Instead of getting caught up in your emotions, you simply observe them with curiosity and compassion. This fosters a non-judgmental relationship with your inner world, allowing you to be more present with your feelings without becoming overwhelmed by them.

Techniques for Grounding Yourself in the Present Moment

Grounding techniques are practices that help you anchor yourself in the present moment, often by connecting to your physical body and the environment around you. These techniques are especially useful when you find yourself feeling overwhelmed, anxious, or disconnected. Grounding helps you re-establish a sense of stability and calm, even in chaotic or stressful situations.

One simple grounding technique involves focusing on your five senses. This practice helps bring your attention away from your thoughts and into the immediate environment. Start by identifying five things you can see around you, then five things you can touch, five things you can hear, and so on. Engaging your senses in this way helps to draw your awareness to the present moment, reducing the tendency to get lost in your thoughts.

Another grounding technique is to focus on your breath while also being aware of your posture and the weight of your body. Sit or stand up straight, placing your feet flat on the ground. Feel the solid support beneath you. Notice the sensation of your body making contact with the earth. By paying attention to the physical sensations of being grounded, you re-establish a sense of presence.

The "5-4-3-2-1" grounding exercise is another powerful method. In this practice, you start by observing five things you can see, four things you can feel, three things you can hear, two things you can smell, and one thing you can taste. This exercise helps distract you from anxious or racing thoughts and brings you back into your body and the world around you. It's particularly effective in moments when you feel scattered or disconnected.

Mindful walking is another excellent grounding technique. As you walk, pay attention to each step and the sensations in your feet, legs, and body. Walk slowly and deliberately, noticing the movement of your body and how your feet make contact with the ground. This simple practice can help you reconnect with the present moment, even if you're walking through a busy environment.

Grounding practices like these can be used at any time during the day, especially when you notice your thoughts drifting away from the present moment or when you're feeling overwhelmed. The more you practice grounding techniques, the easier it becomes to stay rooted in the present moment, no matter what's happening around you.

The Role of Breathwork in Quieting the Mind

Breathwork is one of the most powerful tools for cultivating presence and quieting the mind. The breath is always with us, yet most people are unaware of its profound ability to influence our mental and emotional states. By consciously directing your breath, you can regulate your nervous system, calm anxiety, and enhance your ability to stay present.

The breath acts as a bridge between the body and the mind. When we are stressed or anxious, our breathing tends to become shallow and rapid. This signals to the body that we are in a state of fight-or-flight. Conversely, when we take slow, deep breaths, it activates the parasympathetic nervous system, which helps us relax and return to a state of calm. Breathwork allows us to consciously shift our physiology, bringing us back to the present moment.

One of the simplest and most effective breathwork techniques is deep diaphragmatic breathing. To practice this, sit comfortably with your back straight and place one hand on your chest and the other on your abdomen. As you inhale, focus on expanding your diaphragm, allowing your abdomen to rise. As you exhale, let your abdomen fall back toward your spine. This type of breathing encourages full oxygenation of the body, calming the nervous system and helping you feel more grounded and present.

Another popular breathwork technique is the 4-7-8 breathing method. To practice this, inhale for a count of four, hold your breath for a count of seven, and exhale for a count of eight. This technique slows down the breath, calms the mind, and enhances focus. It's especially helpful if you feel overwhelmed or anxious and need to quickly regain a sense of balance.

Box breathing is another effective method. Inhale for a count of four, hold your breath for four, exhale for four, and hold again for four. Repeat this cycle for several rounds. This technique helps to regulate the breath, reduce anxiety, and bring you back into the present moment by focusing on your breath and the rhythm of your inhale and exhale.

Pranayama, the ancient practice of breath control in yoga, offers numerous other breathwork techniques for cultivating presence and quieting the mind. Techniques like alternate nostril breathing, ujjayi breath (the victorious breath), and kapalbhati (a cleansing breath) can be used to enhance concentration, calm the nervous system, and bring clarity to the mind. Each of these techniques can be adapted to suit your personal needs and preferences.

When practicing breathwork, it's important to remain patient and gentle with yourself. The goal is not to force the breath or to control it in a rigid way, but to develop a connection with your breath and use it as a tool to bring you into the present moment. Over time, as you incorporate breathwork into your daily routine, you'll find it easier to return to a state of calm and presence, no matter the situation.

The practices of guided meditation, grounding techniques, and breathwork are powerful tools for cultivating presence in your life. By incorporating these practices into your daily routine, you can reduce mental clutter, decrease stress, and foster a deeper connection with yourself and the world around you. Each of these practices helps you to step out of the noise of the mind and return to the present moment, where true peace and clarity reside.

Guided meditation allows you to cultivate awareness and detachment from your thoughts, while grounding techniques help you reconnect with your body and the environment around you. Breathwork provides a powerful way to regulate your emotions, calm your nervous system, and return to a state of presence. Together, these practices form a holistic approach to mental and emotional well-being, supporting you on your journey to self-awareness and transformation.

The more consistently you practice these techniques, the easier it becomes to stay present in any situation. As you deepen your connection to the present moment, you'll experience greater mental clarity, emotional balance, and a profound sense of peace.

Living Beyond Constructs

Living beyond mental constructs is not merely an abstract idea, but a profound shift in how we experience and engage with the world. It is the process of freeing oneself from the invisible yet powerful frameworks of thought that dictate how we see ourselves, others, and our lives. These constructs are built from past experiences, societal expectations, and the stories we tell ourselves, and they often trap us in cycles of suffering, confusion, and disconnection. When we learn to live beyond these constructs, we move into a state of inner freedom, clarity, and authentic connection with both ourselves and the world around us.

How to Embody Freedom from Mental Constructs

Embodying freedom from mental constructs begins with recognizing that these thought patterns are not who you are. They are learned behaviors, conditioned responses, and inherited beliefs that shape your perception of reality. By realizing this, you can begin to disidentify with them and create the space needed to experience life without the limitations imposed by mental constructs.

The first step is to cultivate awareness. Awareness allows you to observe your thoughts without becoming entangled in them. It's about seeing the thoughts and beliefs that arise in your mind as passing phenomena, not as truths that define you. This practice of detachment is key to living beyond constructs. When you can observe your thoughts without judgment, you allow yourself the freedom to choose how to respond, rather than reacting automatically based on old patterns.

Another important practice is mindfulness. By engaging fully in the present moment—whether through meditation, conscious breathing, or simply paying attention to what you are doing—you train your mind to be less preoccupied with past stories or future anxieties. Mindfulness helps you break free from the habitual patterns of thought that shape your perception and experience. It is through mindfulness that we become aware of when we are living from our constructs and when we are experiencing true presence.

Once you cultivate the awareness that these constructs are not your true essence, it becomes easier to let go of them. But letting go is not always easy. It requires the willingness to face uncomfortable emotions and the courage to question long-held beliefs. It might mean challenging the narrative you've lived by and confronting parts of yourself that you've hidden or ignored. This is not a one-time event but a continuous process of self-exploration, refinement, and letting go.

The journey of living beyond mental constructs requires patience and self-compassion. It's a process of gradually shedding the layers of conditioning that no longer serve you. With consistent practice, you will find that you begin to experience more freedom, peace, and joy as the grip of your mental constructs loosens.

Practical Ways to Integrate Stillness into Everyday Life

Living beyond mental constructs is deeply connected to the practice of stillness. While moments of deep meditation or reflection are helpful, true transformation occurs when stillness is integrated into daily life. The essence of stillness is not the absence of activity, but the presence and clarity that comes from within, no matter what external circumstances may be.

One powerful way to integrate stillness into your daily life is through conscious breathing. This practice can be done at any time—while waiting in line, walking, working, or even during stressful moments. Simply pause and take a few deep breaths, bringing your attention back to the present moment. As you breathe, bring your awareness to the sensations of the breath entering and leaving your body. This simple act of pausing and breathing connects you with stillness, even amidst the busyness of life.

Another practical way to integrate stillness is through mindful activities. Engaging in everyday tasks with full attention can bring a sense of calm and presence. For instance, washing dishes can become a meditative practice if you focus on the sensation of the water, the texture of the soap, and the act of cleaning. The goal is to bring your full awareness to what you are doing, rather than letting your mind wander into the past or future.

You can also create intentional pauses in your day. Set aside time for moments of silence, whether it's through meditation, taking a walk in nature, or simply sitting quietly without any distractions. These intentional moments of stillness allow you to reconnect with your inner peace and presence, providing clarity and calmness that will permeate the rest of your day.

Stillness can also be cultivated in how you respond to life's challenges. Instead of reacting impulsively, practice pausing before you speak or act. In this pause, you can center yourself, observe your emotions, and choose a response that aligns with your true self, rather than one driven by old patterns and mental constructs. This practice of mindful response, rather than reaction, fosters a sense of inner peace and helps you stay grounded in the present moment.

By incorporating stillness into everyday life, you create a mental and emotional space where you can experience true freedom. It's not about escaping from the world, but about learning to engage with it from a place of clarity and presence.

How Presence Transforms Relationships and Decisions

One of the most profound ways that living beyond mental constructs impacts your life is in the realm of relationships. When you are free from the habitual stories and beliefs that shape your perception of others, you are able to truly see people as they are, without judgment or expectation. This fosters deeper, more authentic connections, as you are no longer projecting your inner mental constructs onto those around you.

Presence in relationships means listening fully without the interference of preconceived notions or judgments. It's about being present for others, offering your full attention and empathy without distractions or assumptions. When you are present in this way, your relationships become more meaningful, as you are engaging with others from a place of genuine connection, rather than through the lens of past experiences or societal labels.

In romantic relationships, for instance, being present allows you to connect with your partner on a deeper level. It means being attuned to their needs and emotions without being clouded by past relationship patterns or expectations. You can communicate more openly and authentically, creating a foundation of trust and understanding.

Presence also transforms your decision-making process. When you are caught in mental constructs, decisions are often influenced by fear, past trauma, or the desire to conform to external expectations. But when you live beyond constructs, you make decisions from a place of clarity and authenticity. You are no longer swayed by external pressure or internal fears, but instead make choices that align with your true values and desires.

Living with presence allows you to act with greater intention and purpose. You are more likely to make decisions that are in alignment with your authentic self, leading to a life that feels more fulfilling and meaningful. You become more attuned to your intuition and inner wisdom, allowing these qualities to guide you, rather than being led by the mental constructs of the mind.

In addition, presence in decision-making fosters a greater sense of peace. When you are no longer attached to outcomes or driven by anxiety about the future, you can make decisions with a sense of calm and ease. You trust that you are making the right choices, not based on fear or doubt, but from a place of confidence and clarity.

Living beyond mental constructs is a profound journey toward freedom, authenticity, and inner peace. By learning to embody freedom from mental constructs, you break free from the patterns of thought that have limited your potential. Practicing stillness in everyday life helps you stay grounded and connected to the present moment, while cultivating deeper awareness of yourself and the world around you.

As you integrate presence into your relationships and decision-making, you experience more authentic connections and choices that reflect your true self. Ultimately, living beyond mental constructs allows you to experience life with greater clarity, peace, and joy, as you are no longer bound by the invisible frameworks that once shaped your reality. Instead, you live in alignment with the present moment, where true freedom resides.

Chapter 6: Embodying Your True Self

Embodying your true self is a journey of deep transformation, where you learn to move beyond the mental constructs that have shaped your identity and embrace the authentic, unfiltered essence of who you truly are. This process involves shedding the layers of societal expectations, past conditioning, and limiting beliefs, and stepping into a life that reflects your deepest values and purpose. It is about aligning your thoughts, actions, and beliefs with the truth of your being, rather than the false stories you've been told or that you have told yourself.

The Essence of Your True Self

Your true self is not defined by labels, roles, or external achievements. It is the core of your being, untouched by the judgment or expectations of others. It is your natural state of being, where you exist beyond the mental constructs that distort your perception of reality. Your true self is the part of you that experiences life directly, without the interference of past narratives or the pressure of future outcomes. It is grounded in the present moment, radiating authenticity, love, and peace.

The key to embodying your true self is to first recognize that you are not the sum of your thoughts, beliefs, or the roles you play in life. These are external aspects of your experience, but they do not define you. Your true self is deeper than your thoughts and beyond the identity that you've created or inherited. When you realize this, you can begin to let go of the need to be someone you are not, and you can stop identifying with the mental constructs that have shaped your sense of self.

Letting Go of Old Constructs

The process of embodying your true self involves a conscious effort to release the mental constructs that no longer serve you. These constructs are often deeply ingrained, shaped by societal expectations, family beliefs, and past experiences. They can include the need for approval, the fear of rejection, the desire for success, and the belief that you must conform to certain standards in order to be loved or accepted.

Letting go of these constructs is not always easy, as they are often tied to deeply held fears and insecurities. But this is the key to liberation—understanding that you do not need to fit into these predefined boxes to be worthy. You are enough as you are. The moment you begin to acknowledge that you have the power to choose which beliefs and stories you hold onto, you start to create space for your true self to emerge.

This process of releasing can be done through various practices, such as mindfulness, journaling, meditation, or therapy. The goal is to become aware of the mental patterns that keep you attached to false identities and to consciously choose to let them go. As you do, you will start to feel a greater sense of peace and clarity, as the weight of these constructs is lifted, allowing your authentic self to shine through.

Aligning with Your Core Values

To truly embody your true self, it is essential to connect with and live in alignment with your core values. Your values are the guiding principles that reflect what is most important to you in life. They are the foundation upon which you can build a life that feels meaningful and fulfilling. When you are aligned with your values, you experience a sense of purpose and inner peace that cannot be found in external achievements or validation.

Start by reflecting on what truly matters to you. What are the qualities you most admire in others? What gives you a sense of fulfillment and joy? Take time to explore your passions, your desires, and your deepest aspirations. Often, the things that light you up are the clearest indicators of your core values.

Once you have identified your values, make a commitment to live by them. This means aligning your daily choices with these values and letting go of anything that does not resonate with your true self. For example, if honesty is a core value for you, practice speaking your truth in all areas of your life. If creativity is important to you, make time for creative expression, whether it's through art, writing, or another form of self-expression.

Living in alignment with your values will bring a sense of fulfillment that cannot be found through external validation or the pursuit of fleeting goals. It will allow you to embody your true self in every area of your life, from your relationships to your work and personal goals.

Embracing the Power of Self-Expression

One of the most powerful ways to embody your true self is through self-expression. When you express yourself authentically, you create an energetic alignment with your true essence. Self-expression can take many forms: through your words, actions, art, career, or relationships. It is the act of showing up in the world as the person you truly are, without fear or hesitation.

Self-expression begins with the courage to be vulnerable. It requires you to let go of the fear of judgment or rejection and trust that your truth is worthy of being shared. Whether it's expressing your emotions, sharing your ideas, or pursuing your passions, self-expression allows you to step fully into who you are and contribute to the world in a meaningful way.

Remember that self-expression is not about perfection or approval—it's about being true to yourself. The more you express your authentic self, the more you will feel connected to your true essence and the people around you. The act of being yourself, unapologetically and without self-doubt, creates a ripple effect that inspires others to do the same.

Practicing Self-Compassion

As you embark on the journey of embodying your true self, it's important to practice self-compassion. This means treating yourself with kindness, understanding, and patience as you navigate the process of self-discovery and transformation. Embracing your true self can bring up a lot of emotions, including fear, shame, or self-doubt. It's essential to approach these emotions with love and acceptance, rather than judgment.

Self-compassion is a practice that helps you stay grounded and centered as you move through challenges. It encourages you to be gentle with yourself when you make mistakes or face setbacks. Remember, embodying your true self is a continuous journey, not a destination. There will be moments of growth, discomfort, and learning along the way. By practicing self-compassion, you allow yourself to embrace each step of the process with grace and patience.

Living Authentically and Without Fear

Finally, embodying your true self means living authentically, without the fear of being judged or rejected. It's about embracing who you are, unapologetically and fully, and trusting that the world will meet you with the same authenticity. When you live authentically, you attract the people, opportunities, and experiences that are aligned with your true self.

Living authentically also means taking risks. It may require you to step outside of your comfort zone, challenge societal expectations, and make bold decisions that align with your heart's desires. While this can be intimidating, it is through these courageous actions that you fully embody your true self.

In the end, embodying your true self is about living with integrity, embracing your unique qualities, and letting go of the need to be anything other than who you are. It is a journey of liberation—one that allows you to step into your full potential and live a life that reflects your deepest truth.

By embodying your true self, you create a life of authenticity, purpose, and inner peace. This is the life you were always meant to live, and it is available to you now. It's time to step into your power and become the person you've always been, beneath the layers of mental constructs and false identities.

What It Means to Be Free of Mental Constructs

True freedom comes from the liberation of the mind—freedom from the mental constructs that confine us, limit our potential, and cloud our perception of reality. When we free ourselves from these mental structures, we begin to experience life in its purest form, as we connect more deeply with our true selves, our surroundings, and the world. Freedom from mental constructs is not merely a philosophical idea, but a profound shift in consciousness that can completely transform the way we live, think, and interact with the world.

In this section, we'll explore what it truly means to be free from mental constructs, the characteristics of a liberated mind, signs of transformation and growth, and how this freedom impacts our daily lives.

The Characteristics of a Liberated Mind

A liberated mind is not burdened by the weight of limiting beliefs, outdated narratives, or social expectations. It operates from a place of clarity, openness, and flexibility. The characteristics of a liberated mind are profound and deeply transformative. Below are key attributes that define a liberated mind:

A liberated mind is characterized by clarity and awareness. When free from mental constructs, the mind is not cluttered by unnecessary thoughts or self-doubt. It is aware of its thoughts but is not attached to them. This clarity allows for better decision-making, as the individual can think critically without being swayed by internal bias or preconceived notions. The mind becomes a tool for creativity and insight rather than a source of stress or confusion.

A mind free from mental constructs is deeply anchored in the present moment. It is not preoccupied with past regrets or future anxieties. The individual experiences life as it is, without the filter of judgment, interpretation, or comparison. Presence is key to this liberation, allowing for a deeper appreciation of each moment and a richer, more meaningful engagement with life.

Freedom from mental constructs also leads to emotional liberation. When the mind is no longer tethered to limiting beliefs, such as "I am not good enough" or "I must be perfect," emotional patterns begin to shift. Emotions no longer have a hold over the individual. Instead of reacting impulsively to triggers, a liberated mind is able to observe emotions without judgment, allowing them to flow and pass without resistance. This emotional freedom contributes to greater peace and emotional balance.

A liberated mind has no attachment to its identity, achievements, or material possessions. This doesn't mean that it rejects these things, but rather that it no longer relies on them for validation or a sense of worth. The mind becomes flexible and adaptable, understanding that the only constant in life is change. A person with a liberated mind is free from the need to control, manipulate, or hold on to anything, embracing life as it comes.

One of the most important characteristics of a liberated mind is unconditional self-acceptance. Free from the constructs that society, family, and even the individual self have imposed, the mind can fully embrace who it is without needing to prove anything. This acceptance leads to greater self-love, confidence, and compassion. The individual no longer seeks external validation but feels an internal sense of worth.

With the shedding of limiting beliefs, the mind becomes open to new ideas and experiences. It no longer operates from a place of fear or rigidity but is curious and eager to explore life with fresh eyes. A liberated mind seeks growth and learning, welcoming challenges as opportunities for expansion and self-discovery.

Signs of Transformation and Growth

When you begin to break free from mental constructs, the transformation may not be immediate or dramatic, but it is profound and noticeable. Here are several signs that indicate you are undergoing transformation and growth:

One of the most immediate signs of freedom from mental constructs is a deep sense of inner peace. As you release the mental narratives that have held you back—fear, anxiety, self-criticism, and limiting beliefs—you begin to feel more at ease in your own skin. The constant chatter of the mind quiets, and you experience a profound sense of calm. This peace is not circumstantial but comes from within.

As mental constructs fall away, judgment—both of yourself and others—begins to dissolve. You stop seeing the world through the lens of right and wrong, good and bad, or better and worse. Instead, you begin to see things as they are, free from the filters of judgment and expectation. This shift leads to greater empathy, understanding, and tolerance for yourself and others.

Another sign of transformation is an increased sense of fearlessness. When mental constructs no longer control your actions, you feel free to pursue your passions and desires without hesitation. The fear of failure, judgment, or rejection no longer holds you back. You take risks, knowing that your worth is not dependent on the outcome, but on the courage to follow your heart.

People who have freed themselves from mental constructs are able to embrace change with openness and resilience. They understand that change is a natural part of life and that their identity is not tied to any particular outcome or state of being. Rather than resisting change or clinging to the past, they flow with life, accepting the ebb and flow of experiences with grace.

As you become free from the need to conform to external expectations, you start expressing yourself authentically. You no longer feel the pressure to please others or fit into predefined molds. Instead, you act, speak, and live according to your true nature, unafraid to stand out or go against the grain. This authenticity fosters deeper connections with others and creates a more fulfilling and honest way of living.

A liberated mind experiences a deepening sense of compassion and understanding for others. When we let go of our own mental constructs and judgments, we naturally extend this compassion to those around us. We recognize that others, too, are suffering from their own limiting beliefs and mental constructs, and we feel a deep empathy for their struggles. This compassion extends not only to others but also to ourselves, fostering a sense of interconnectedness.

How Freedom from Constructs Impacts Daily Living

When you free yourself from mental constructs, the impact on your daily life is nothing short of transformative. Here are some of the ways this freedom affects the way you live:

Freedom from mental constructs allows you to experience relationships in a more genuine and compassionate way. Since you are no longer operating from a place of fear, expectation, or judgment, you are able to connect with others on a deeper, more authentic level. You no longer project your insecurities or try to control the relationship, but instead, you embrace each person as they are, free from the need for approval.

With fewer distractions from the mind's constant chatter, a liberated mind is able to focus more fully on the task at hand. The clarity and present-moment awareness that come with freedom from mental constructs make it easier to stay engaged and productive in daily activities. Whether at work, home, or in creative pursuits, the ability to focus and immerse yourself in the moment leads to more effective and fulfilling work.

As mental constructs are dismantled, creativity flows more freely. The mind is no longer bogged down by limiting beliefs and judgments, and it is able to think more expansively. Whether in art, problem-solving, or innovation, a liberated mind opens the door to new ideas and possibilities. The freedom to think outside the box and explore different perspectives leads to a more fulfilling and dynamic creative process.

With the ability to observe thoughts and emotions without attachment, decision-making becomes easier and more intuitive. A liberated mind is not clouded by fear, doubt, or past experiences, allowing for more clear and effective choices. The flexibility to adapt to changing circumstances and consider multiple options with an open mind leads to better decisions.

Freedom from mental constructs allows you to connect with your true desires and passions. Without the need to conform to external expectations, you begin to make choices that align with your authentic self. This brings a sense of purpose and fulfillment, as you live in alignment with your values and passions, rather than living for approval or external validation.

In conclusion, being free from mental constructs is a powerful and transformative experience that impacts every aspect of your life. It allows you to live more authentically, express yourself freely, and connect with others on a deeper level. As you cultivate freedom from these constructs, you begin to experience a life of greater peace, creativity, and purpose, and the world around you begins to reflect this newfound sense of liberation. The journey towards freedom is ongoing, but the rewards of a liberated mind are immeasurable.

Practical Steps for Sustained Transformation

Achieving sustained transformation requires not only the initial steps of awareness and release but also a commitment to continuous growth and evolution. Transformation is an ongoing process that requires dedication, mindfulness, and the right tools to maintain progress. In this section, we will explore practical steps for ensuring that the transformation you have experienced remains sustainable, how to create a personal plan for ongoing growth, and identify resources that can help support you in your journey toward sustained transformation.

How to Maintain Awareness and Avoid Falling Back

The key to maintaining sustained transformation is awareness. Transformation is a process that often requires a shift in your mindset, behavior, and the way you perceive the world. While these shifts may initially feel like significant changes, it's easy to slip back into old patterns when life becomes challenging or the excitement of change begins to fade. To maintain the awareness you've cultivated, here are some important practices:

Consistent Mindfulness Practice

Mindfulness is a powerful tool for sustaining transformation. It keeps you anchored in the present moment and aware of your thoughts, emotions, and actions. By regularly practicing mindfulness, you can prevent old, unhelpful mental constructs from creeping back into your daily life. Start by setting aside time each day for mindfulness practices like meditation, breathwork, or simply paying attention to the present moment. Whether it's through guided meditations, mindful walking, or body scan techniques, make mindfulness a non-negotiable part of your routine.

Journaling for Reflection

Journaling is another tool that helps maintain awareness. Writing down your thoughts, feelings, and reflections allows you to process experiences and track your progress. It's important to note both your successes and setbacks in this practice. Regular journaling can help you recognize when old patterns or limiting beliefs are resurfacing and can provide you with insights into why this might be happening. Reflecting on your journey and staying connected to your inner self through journaling can strengthen your commitment to growth and transformation.

Self-Observation and Accountability

Self-observation is about being the observer of your own life—detached from judgment but present with your thoughts and actions. You can do this by checking in with yourself regularly throughout the day. What thoughts are you holding onto? Are you slipping back into old patterns? By being aware of your thoughts and actions in real-time, you are more likely to catch yourself before you fall back into negative habits. Consider finding an accountability partner—a friend, mentor, or coach—to help you stay on track. Sharing your journey with someone who understands and supports you can provide valuable encouragement and feedback.

Reaffirm Your Intentions

Transformation begins with a clear intention, and it is essential to continue reaffirming that intention even after you've made progress. Revisit the reasons why you started this journey and remind yourself regularly of your goals. You can do this by writing them down, visualizing them, or saying affirmations that resonate with your deeper purpose. Reaffirming your intentions helps you stay motivated and keeps you focused on the bigger picture rather than on temporary setbacks.

Create Boundaries with Negative Influences

Often, falling back into old patterns occurs because of external influences—negative people, environments, or situations that challenge your transformation. It's important to recognize these influences and set healthy boundaries. This may mean limiting your contact with people who drag you down or removing yourself from environments that foster negative thinking. Cultivating supportive relationships and surrounding yourself with people who encourage growth can help you stay grounded in your new mindset.

Creating a Personal Plan for Continuous Growth

Sustained transformation requires a long-term approach. While awareness is key to maintaining transformation, having a clear plan for continuous growth can help you keep progressing. A personal growth plan is a roadmap that helps you stay on course and ensures that you're always moving toward higher levels of consciousness and personal fulfillment.

Set Clear, Achievable Goals

Your personal growth plan should be grounded in clearly defined goals. These goals may relate to specific areas of your life, such as emotional health, career, relationships, or personal well-being. The goals should be achievable and measurable. For example, instead of saying "I want to be more confident," you could set a specific goal such as "I will speak up in meetings at work at least once per week" or "I will practice self-compassion by saying three positive affirmations each morning." Breaking larger goals into smaller, actionable steps makes the process more manageable and helps you stay focused.

Track Progress and Adjust

A key aspect of a successful growth plan is tracking your progress. Keep a record of your achievements, challenges, and lessons learned along the way. Regularly review your progress to see how far you've come and identify areas where you can improve. If you notice that you've slipped into old habits, take time to reassess your plan and make adjustments. Growth is not a straight line; it's a journey with highs and lows. What matters most is your ability to keep moving forward.

Continue Learning and Expanding Your Knowledge

Transformation involves expanding your mind and heart,

and this is a lifelong process. Make it a priority to continue learning about new practices, perspectives, and ideas that can help you grow. Read books, attend workshops, take courses, or listen to podcasts that resonate with your journey. Seek out information that challenges your current way of thinking and helps you break free from limiting beliefs. Knowledge is a powerful tool for growth, and the more you know, the more equipped you will be to navigate the challenges that arise along the way.

Create Rituals for Personal Development

Incorporating daily rituals and practices into your routine can provide structure and stability to your growth plan. Rituals can include meditation, affirmations, journaling, exercise, or even creating a morning routine that sets a positive tone for the day. These rituals help reinforce the mindset of continuous growth and provide opportunities for reflection, self-care, and inner alignment. The key to these rituals is consistency—they don't need to be long or complicated, but they should be something that you can commit to on a daily or weekly basis.

Celebrate Milestones

A growth plan is not just about the destination—it's about the journey. Celebrate your milestones, no matter how big or small. Every step you take toward becoming your true self is worth acknowledging. Celebrating milestones keeps you motivated and gives you a sense of accomplishment, which can help you sustain the momentum you've built. Take time to reflect on your growth and acknowledge the hard work you've put in.

Resources and Tools for Ongoing Support

As you continue on your journey of transformation, it's important to equip yourself with the resources and tools that will support you along the way. These resources can be books, courses, meditation apps, therapy, or even support groups. Here are some key tools to help you maintain and nurture your transformation:

Books and Podcasts

Books and podcasts are invaluable resources for personal growth. Seek out books that inspire you and challenge your way of thinking. Some classic texts on transformation include "The Power of Now" by Eckhart Tolle, "The Four Agreements" by Don Miguel Ruiz, and "Radical Acceptance" by Tara Brach. Podcasts like "The Tim Ferriss Show," "The Minimalists," and "The Life Coach School Podcast" are excellent sources of insight, wisdom, and practical advice for personal development.

Meditation Apps and Mindfulness Tools

Apps like Headspace, Calm, or Insight Timer offer guided meditations, mindfulness exercises, and tools to help you stay grounded and connected to the present moment. These tools can support your efforts to maintain awareness, reduce stress, and create space for stillness in your life. Meditation can be an excellent way to deepen your connection to your true self and support ongoing transformation.

Coaching or Therapy

Having a coach or therapist to guide you through your transformation can be extremely helpful. Whether you choose to work with a coach who specializes in personal development or a therapist who can help you navigate deep emotional work, having a professional by your side can provide the support and accountability you need to stay on track. Therapy or coaching can also help you work through obstacles, challenge limiting beliefs, and navigate the ups and downs of personal growth.

Support Groups and Communities

Joining a support group or community of like-minded individuals can provide an additional layer of support. Sharing your journey with others who are also committed to personal growth can offer encouragement, wisdom, and motivation. There are many online and in-person communities dedicated to personal development, mindfulness, and transformation. These groups can be a source of inspiration and provide a sense of belonging as you continue to grow and evolve.

Journaling Prompts and Exercises

Regular journaling is an essential part of the transformation process. Using specific prompts and exercises can help guide your self-reflection and deepen your understanding of yourself. Prompts such as "What limiting beliefs am I still holding on to?" or "What am I grateful for today?" can help you uncover patterns in your thinking and give you new perspectives on your growth. Journaling is a tool that you can use to measure your progress and stay connected to your inner truth.

Sustained transformation is a lifelong process that requires commitment, discipline, and the right tools. By maintaining awareness, creating a personalized growth plan, and utilizing the resources that support your development, you can continue to evolve and embody your true self. The journey may have its ups and downs, but with dedication and persistence, you can create lasting change that leads to a more fulfilled and authentic life.

Building a Life of Inner Freedom

Inner freedom is the ultimate goal of personal transformation. It goes beyond temporary moments of clarity or peace—it's a sustained state where your actions align with your authentic self, your interactions with others reflect your growth, and your life embodies a sense of fulfillment and harmony. Building a life of inner freedom involves deep introspection, intentional living, and a commitment to staying true to yourself. This section explores how to align your actions with your authentic self, the impact of personal transformation on others, and what it means to live a life of peace and fulfillment.

Aligning Actions with Your Authentic Self

The foundation of inner freedom lies in authenticity. When your actions, decisions, and goals align with who you truly are, life feels more effortless, meaningful, and grounded. However, this alignment requires a clear understanding of your core values, desires, and truths.

Discovering Your Core Values

The first step in aligning with your authentic self is identifying your core values. Core values are the principles that guide your decisions and give your life meaning. They reflect what matters most to you—whether that's integrity, creativity, compassion, or growth. Take time to reflect on your values by asking yourself questions like:

- What qualities do I admire most in others?
- What experiences in life have felt most fulfilling or meaningful?
- What beliefs or principles do I refuse to compromise on?

Understanding your values creates a compass for navigating life's challenges and opportunities. When your actions are rooted in these values, you'll find it easier to stay true to yourself even when external pressures arise.

Living with Intentionality

Authenticity thrives in intentional living. This means making conscious choices that reflect your values and desires rather than acting out of habit, fear, or societal expectations. Intentionality can be as simple as pausing before making a decision to ask, "Does this align with who I am and what I value?" For example, choosing a career path, relationships, or daily routines that align with your passions and values creates a sense of purpose and freedom.

Breaking Free from External Validation

Inner freedom also involves letting go of the need for external validation. Many people live their lives seeking approval from others, which often leads to decisions that feel misaligned with their true selves. Building a life of inner freedom means trusting your inner voice more than the opinions of others. It's about prioritizing self-acceptance over societal standards. Ask yourself:

- Am I making this choice because it feels right for me, or because I want to please others?
- Does this action bring me closer to my authentic self?

By consistently choosing authenticity over approval, you strengthen your sense of self and create a life that feels genuinely fulfilling.

The Ripple Effect of Personal Transformation on Others

Personal transformation is not an isolated experience—it inevitably impacts those around you. When you live authentically, you inspire others to do the same. Your growth creates a ripple effect, influencing relationships, communities, and even the larger world.

Leading by Example

The most powerful way to inspire others is by embodying the principles you value. When you live with authenticity, compassion, and purpose, others notice. Your actions become a silent invitation for those around you to reflect on their own lives and consider how they might align with their true selves. This is especially important in close relationships, where your transformation can inspire loved ones to explore their own potential for growth and freedom.

Fostering Healthier Relationships

As you let go of mental constructs and embrace inner freedom, your relationships naturally improve. Freeing yourself from expectations and judgments allows you to approach others with greater empathy and understanding. When you no longer project your own insecurities onto others or cling to preconceived notions about them, your interactions become more genuine. Healthy relationships thrive on authenticity, and your transformation can create deeper, more meaningful connections with those you care about.

Creating a Positive Impact on Communities

The ripple effect extends beyond personal relationships. A transformed individual often becomes a catalyst for positive change within their community. Whether it's through acts of kindness, advocacy for important causes, or simply radiating a sense of calm and balance, your personal growth contributes to the well-being of those around you. Imagine the collective impact if more people embraced inner freedom and authenticity—the world would undoubtedly be a more compassionate and harmonious place.

A Vision for Living a Life of Peace and Fulfillment

Inner freedom ultimately leads to a life of peace and fulfillment. This vision is not about escaping challenges or achieving perfection but about cultivating a deep sense of contentment and purpose, regardless of external circumstances.

Embracing Impermanence

One of the keys to living a life of peace is accepting impermanence. Change is an inevitable part of life, and clinging to the idea of stability often leads to suffering. Inner freedom allows you to navigate change with grace, knowing that your true self remains constant even as external situations evolve. By letting go of attachments and expectations, you create space for new experiences and opportunities to unfold naturally.

Practicing Gratitude

Gratitude is a powerful tool for cultivating fulfillment. When you focus on what you have rather than what you lack, your perspective shifts from scarcity to abundance. Make gratitude a daily practice by reflecting on the positive aspects of your life, no matter how small. Over time, this practice rewires your mindset to notice and appreciate the beauty and opportunities that surround you.

Living in Alignment with Purpose

Living a life of peace and fulfillment also means aligning with your purpose. Purpose doesn't have to be a grand mission—it can be as simple as contributing to the well-being of others, pursuing your passions, or nurturing meaningful relationships. When your actions align with your purpose, life feels more satisfying and purposeful.

Nurturing Self-Compassion

A life of peace and fulfillment is rooted in self-compassion.

Transformation is a journey filled with ups and downs, and it's important to treat yourself with kindness along the way. When setbacks occur, remind yourself that growth takes time and that self-acceptance is a vital part of the process. By embracing your imperfections, you free yourself from the unrealistic pressure to be perfect and allow room for genuine growth.

Prioritizing Presence

Finally, a fulfilled life is one lived in the present moment. Inner freedom enables you to let go of regrets about the past and worries about the future, anchoring you in the here and now. Presence allows you to fully experience life's joys and challenges, fostering a sense of connection to yourself and the world around you.

Building a life of inner freedom is a transformative journey that requires commitment, self-awareness, and intentional action. By aligning your actions with your authentic self, embracing the ripple effect of your transformation, and envisioning a life of peace and fulfillment, you can create a reality that feels deeply aligned with your true nature. Inner freedom is not just a destination—it's a way of being, one that continually evolves as you grow and expand into your fullest potential.

Closing Thoughts

As we come to the end of this journey, take a moment to reflect on how far you've come. Writing this book has been a labor of love, and it's my hope that its pages have inspired, challenged, and supported you on your path to inner freedom. Remember, this journey is not about achieving perfection but about peeling back the layers of mental constructs to uncover the true, limitless essence of who you are.

You now hold the tools and insights to navigate life with greater clarity, compassion, and purpose. But this is just the beginning. Transformation is a lifelong process—an ever-unfolding journey of growth, awareness, and connection. There will be days when old patterns resurface or when challenges feel overwhelming, and that's okay. Growth isn't linear, but every small step you take toward self-awareness creates ripples of change.

Embodying your true self means living with courage, authenticity, and presence. It means showing up for yourself, making conscious choices, and letting go of what no longer serves you. As you continue forward, trust in your ability to create a life that aligns with your deepest truths.

Thank you for allowing me to be a part of your transformation. The world needs more people who are awake, authentic, and at peace with themselves. As you embrace your freedom, may you inspire others to do the same.

This isn't just the end of a book—it's the beginning of a brighter, more authentic chapter of your life. Take it one moment at a time, knowing you are always capable of growth, love, and liberation. You've got this.